D1489068

HOW TO BE A FREELANCE WRITER

Also by David Martindale

Earth Shelters

A GUIDE TO BUILDING A FULL-TIME CAREER

DAVID MARTINDALE

HOW TO BE A FREELANCE WRITER

CROWN PUBLISHERS, INC.
NEW YORK

Inquiries should be addressed to Crown Publishers, Inc., One Park Avenue, New York, New York 10016

Printed in the United States of America

Published simultaneously in Canada by General Publishing Company Limited

Library of Congress Cataloging in Publication Data

Martindale, David.
    How to be a freelance writer.

    Includes index.
    1. Authorship.   I. Title.
PN151.M28 1982 808'.02   82-2498
ISBN: 0-517-547856   AACR2

10 9 8 7 6 5 4 3 2 1

First Edition

Contents

Preface

When I began my freelance writing career in 1975, I did what many would-be writers do: I bought several of the leading how-to books, the ones written by the established freelancers. At the time, those books seemed quite helpful. In fact, after reading each of them thoroughly, I was convinced I knew just about everything I needed to know about the tantalizing profession of freelance writing.

I was wrong.

When I look back on the last seven years, I realize that most of the knowledge I've acquired about my career was gained not from those books but from ordinary trial and error. What's more, not one of those how-to books gave me any indication what it's *really* like to be a full-time freelance writer. From what I had read, I expected freelancing would be some sort of razzle-dazzle, action-packed adventure movie in which I would play a starring role, always riding into yet another sunset in the final frame, joyously clutching another acceptance notice high above my head. No one ever told me about the rejection, the disappointment, and the all-too-frequent phantom checks that editors insisted had been mailed weeks ago.

Although I didn't realize it when I began my career, nearly all freelancing how-to books share one common fault: they gloss over the drawbacks of the profession. Instead, most promise the reader a torrid romance with the twin gods, Fame and Fortune, if only the reader is willing to follow the author's simple prescription for success.

If only there *were* no drawbacks to freelancing. If only there *were* simple prescriptions for success.

I have little tolerance for authors who deliberately downplay the negative aspects of their careers just to make a buck. In my opinion, telling a reader only what he wants to hear is almost as dishonest as telling a blatant lie. Nor do I subscribe to the "Gee whiz, isn't it a wonderful world" school of writing. Such shameless hype belongs on Madison Avenue, not in a how-to book that may profoundly influence the reader's future.

By the same token, I don't believe in taking cheap shots at any profession just for the sake of raising the reader's eyebrows, least of all a profession that I've personally found both challenging and modestly profitable. But I do believe in balance—in telling the bad with the good. I believe in being objective—and that's what *this* how-to book is all about.

Clearly, I can't begin to recount *all* the information you'll need in order to pursue your freelance career. You're still going to have to endure a great deal of trial and error. This book is merely one man's insights into his profession, sans the rose-colored glasses and promises of a pot of gold at the end of the rainbow.

This book does not deal with lofty theories and ponderous abstractions. Instead, it offers nitty-gritty, over-the-shoulder, useful advice from someone who has firsthand knowledge of what it's like to go from an aspiring freelancer to a full-time pro.

How to Be a Freelance Writer is intended primarily for those who aspire to make a living by writing magazine articles. I can't guarantee you'll achieve that goal, but if that's your aim, I can help you try. Even if you'd rather just dabble in freelancing, writing an occasional article, you can still benefit from this book by skipping the first and last sections and focusing on Part 2, "The Profession of Freelancing." And if you already have a few magazine articles to your credit and you're anxious to pursue the career full time, this book offers some solid tips on how to do just that. If, while you're reading, you come across a subject with which you're already familiar, just skip over that material and move on to the next section.

Still, no matter what your purpose for reading this book, a word of caution: you're not going to be pleased by everything you read in the following pages. After all, the truth *can* hurt. So if you find I manage to destroy a dream, deflate a myth, or dash a hope . . . well, I'm sorry, but at least I warned you. My no-nonsense, tell-it-like-it-is approach may not always send your spirits soaring, but at least you can take some comfort in the fact that I'm telling you *both* sides of the freelancing story.

In the long run, such honesty will prove far more helpful to you *and* your career than a shelf full of pie-in-the-sky fables.

1 | THE LURE OF FREELANCING

1 The Life of a Freelance Writer: The Glamour and the Gloom

Suppose a friend invites you to a cocktail party. The two of you mingle with the guests, exchanging the usual pleasantries and, in the course of the evening, you're introduced to five people: an accountant, a dermatologist, a schoolteacher, a florist, and a freelance writer. Just before you leave the party, your friend turns to you and asks, "Of the five people you just met, which one has the most glamorous occupation?" How would you respond?

Chances are you'd choose the freelance writer.

Of course, your choice is hardly surprising. The fact that you've decided to read this book—as opposed to *War and Peace* or *Valley of the Dolls*, for example—is a good indication that you're seriously considering freelancing as a profession. And even if you are totally content working at another occupation, there's a good chance you still would have chosen freelance writing as the most glamorous profession. After all, there's nothing particularly fascinating about balancing ledgers, diagnosing skin conditions, grading a spelling exam, or arranging bouquets. Each is a perfectly respectable occupation, to be sure, but hardly the stuff of glamour.

A career as a freelance writer, on the other hand . . . well, that's something entirely different, at least to most nonwriters, anyway. Never mind that most freelance writers never achieve wide recognition, never hobnob with the jet set, and never unwind at the villa of their dreams in Acapulco. Regardless of the fact that most freelancers can't even make a living at their craft, there's

3

still a certain mystique surrounding the profession.
Why?

AH, THE WRITING LIFE

To begin with, writing is one of the world's oldest and most
respected professions. Long before Fitzgerald, Hemingway, and
Michener ever reached for their first dictionaries, authors such
as Virgil, Aristotle, and Dante penned their classic epics. Writing
articles for magazines—even top national publications—by no
means propels a freelancer into the lofty ranks of the literary
greats. Nevertheless, one reason people find the profession so
downright fascinating is because it evokes images of well-known
writers whose works have become legendary.

Another reason freelance writers are held in such high esteem
is envy. Although nearly everyone dreams of writing the Great
American Novel, most people (when pressed, at least) will admit
to being poor writers. And little wonder: writing is fast becoming
a dying art. Largely due to the pervasive influence of television,
Johnny is lucky if he can read, let alone write. Tragically, Johnny's
parents often fare no better, seldom bothering to tackle any writing
project more difficult than compiling a grocery list.

Still, although most people don't try to *pretend* they can write,
too many bureaucrats, scientists, and university professors delude
themselves into thinking they can—not that commoners such as
you or I are able to comprehend their twentieth-century hiero-
glyphics. How could we? Jargon is substituted for ordinary speech,
verbiage for conciseness. It's as though each author had taken a
secret pledge never to use any word containing less than five
syllables. When a freelance writer comes along who can present
a complex, technical subject in language anyone can understand . . . *voilà!* he's heralded as a literary Houdini.

Yet nonwriters not only envy a freelancer's ability to write
lucidly on a wide variety of subjects, they also envy a freelancer's
life-style. "What did *you* do today?" friends will often ask me.
Usually, my response is confined to a single word: work—which
for me means researching or writing. But, occasionally, I do have
to admit I spent the better part of the day riding my bicycle or

running errands. Invariably, such a reply evokes an envious "Must be nice." Of course, I try to explain that on many nights I work well past midnight on an article that may never earn me a penny, let alone be published. But all too often, such explanations fall on deaf ears. To the disgruntled office worker who'd rather spend his days cruising the high seas than cursing his boss, a freelancer has it made.

If only we did.

THE MYSTIQUE DEBUNKED

Let's face it—there's no such thing as an ideal profession. Freelance writing is just like any other career: it has its advantages and its disadvantages. And before you decide whether or not to pursue the career, you owe it to yourself to become thoroughly familiar with both.

What follows is a no-holds-barred, tell-it-like-it-is listing of the pros and cons of trying to become a full-time freelance writer. Quite obviously, this list is hardly definitive. It's not gospel, but merely one writer's highly subjective opinion. Still, the following several paragraphs should give you a better perspective on the freelancing profession.

So here goes.

First, the good news. The advantages to becoming a freelance writer are

You don't need any formal training. There are no degrees to earn, no exams to pass, no licenses to obtain. Most editors couldn't care less whether you graduated from grammar school, let alone Northwestern University's School of Journalism. All they're concerned about is your writing ability, your accuracy, your professionalism, and your ideas—period.

You're your own boss. There's never anyone standing over your shoulder telling you what to do. You determine what you write, how much you write, and for what publications you wish to write. The ultimate arbiter of your career is you, not someone else.

Your time is your own. You have deadlines, of course, but by and large, you can kiss the rat race good-bye. You can forget about squeezing aboard crowded subways or hassling with rush-hour traffic. As a freelancer, you don't have to commute. Nor do you have to lock yourself into a nine-to-five schedule (unless, or course, that's the type of schedule you prefer). You can begin writing at 6:00 A.M. and call it a day by 2:00 P.M., or you can sleep until noon and stay up writing all night long. It's entirely up to you. Best of all, on those quiet Monday mornings when everyone else has gloomily returned to work, you can run your errands, visit your dentist, or take a stroll in the park—whatever *you* decide to do.

You can gain access to people and places that you wouldn't ordinarily be able to obtain in other professions. Depending upon the topics you research, you can arrange face-to-face interviews with well-known scientists, movie stars, business tycoons, even congressmen. And frequently, your research will allow you to pay on-site visits to such off-limits places as nuclear power plants, prisons, airport control towers, or offshore oil rigs.

You can develop an expertise in one or more areas. Unlike a newspaper reporter, for example, you can write about subjects which interest *you*, rather than an assignment editor. Eventually, you'll probably develop at least one area of specialization. Once you've established your reputation as an expert in a field, you won't have to contact as many magazines—*editors* will begin contacting *you*.

You can satisfy your craving for self-expression. A magazine article is more than just a dry, lifeless collection of facts strung together in a readable manner. Your own ideas, your own values, your own writing style, will pervade each piece you write. You can jump on a soapbox, expose a scam, profile a personality, or eloquently detail the last hours of a dying child. Each article will present a different challenge—a different outlet for your creative energies.

Okay. So there you have it: the *good* news. Now brace yourself. Grit your teeth and take a deep breath, because now it's time for the *bad* news.

The *dis*advantages of becoming a full-time freelance writer are

The pay stinks. And since few magazines raise their rates to compensate for inflation, the pay's actually getting worse, not better. True, a handful of top national magazines pay $2,000 or more for a single article, but few freelancers ever crack such competitive markets. Most settle for far less lucrative sales, usually just a few hundred dollars per article—often less. Little wonder there are only about two- to three-hundred freelance writers in the entire country able to make a living solely by writing magazine articles. That's right—just two to three hundred!

In 1981, Columbia University's Center for Social Sciences queried 2,239 American authors—men and women who had published at least one book. Their findings: the *average* author earned just $4,775 per year from writing (and these people were writing *books*, not magazine articles!). Even this figure was skewed toward the high side by the top 5 percent of authors who earned more than $80,000 annually. More than half those surveyed had to hold down paid jobs to subsidize their writing. No comparable survey has ever focused on freelancers who write magazine articles, but you can be certain that, financially, freelancers fare even more poorly than the authors in the Columbia study.

Benefits are nonexistent. Forget about retirement programs, profit sharing, employer-paid health insurance, and the oven-stuffer turkey at Christmas. Magazines may provide such benefits to their salaried employees, but not to you. You're freelance, re-member? Your relationship with magazines is solely on a con-tractual basis. Payment, yes; benefits, no!

Payment is sporadic. One week the mailman drops six checks in your mailbox. Suddenly you're rich. But before you make a down payment on a backyard swimming pool, you should realize it may take a couple of months or more before you see another check. A top-notch publication such as *Reader's Digest* pays within five working days after acceptance of a manuscript. But other magazines may take weeks, even months before they get around to mailing your checks. Some refuse to pay you a cent until your article is actually published. Occasionally, you even have to become your own collection agency. I once had to wait a solid year before the financially ailing—and now mercifully defunct—*Argosy* finally paid me for my article. And the only reason they *did* pay was because I went to New York and sat in their lobby until someone handed me the check. Amount owed: just $400.

You have to reinvest at least part of your earnings in your career. The old adage is true: it *takes* money to *make* money. If you're really serious about pursuing the occupation, you must be willing to shell out money for the essentials: a typewriter, office supplies, magazine subcriptions, postage, and travel expenses, to name a few. You can save a bit at tax time by writing off such investments, but the initial capital outlay still has to come from your own pocket—no small expense when you're just getting started.

The competition is stiff. You may never meet another freelancer face-to-face, but rest assured, there are plenty of us out there. Despite the lack of financial incentives, a great many people want to pursue a career in freelance writing. In fact, this is one reason why the pay *is* so low—it's a buyer's market. In the struggle to get ahead, there's always *someone* willing to write an article for a pittance. And you can bet your thesaurus there's sure as hell more than one freelancer anxious to write for *Playboy*,—and every other top magazine.

You not only have to be a writer, but a skilled marketing manager. Contrary to popular opinion, a freelancer does more than just research and write. When just starting out, you can spend a great many hours trying to keep abreast of constantly changing markets, searching for magazines with high sales potential. Fail to pay attention to the markets and your income dwindles to a trickle. Spend too much time plotting marketing strategy and you won't have any spare time to write.

In writer/editor relationships, editors almost always have the upper hand. Certainly most editors are intelligent, reasonably competent, and fair. But not surprisingly, some have no business even working in the profession. Occasionally, editors deliberately delay payments, renege on promises, butcher manuscripts, and even steal ideas. Although you're tempted to "strike back," a freelancer's options are few. Usually, your only recourse is to complain as loudly as you can and make it a point never to write for the offending magazine again.

The job is lonely. It's a cliché, to be sure. But whereas researching an article may give you the chance to meet interesting people, the actual *writing* of the article has to be done alone. No one collaborates with you on the final project. Friends and family can empathize with your ordeal, but they can't do your writing for you. Ultimately, it's just you, the typewriter, and that blank sheet of paper.

It takes a long time to become established in the field. No matter how talented you are, you're not going to be able to quit your job tomorrow and earn enough money your first year to eke out even a poverty-level existence. Unless Aunt Flora dies tomorrow and—God bless her—leaves you a hefty inheritance, you'll either have to continue at your present job and write in your spare time, or else you'll have to take a part-time job to supplement your writing income. Realistically, it will take at least three years—and probably longer—before you'll be able to enter freelancing full time, if at all. The statistics argue that you may *never* earn enough from your writing to pursue freelancing on a full-time basis.

NOW WHAT?

No doubt by this time, some of you are saying, "My God— he must be exaggerating. It can't possibly be that bad."

Sad to say, I'm not exaggerating. Yes, Virginia, it *is* that bad. Take it from someone who knows—firsthand.

So what's your decision? Do the cons outweigh the pros? If so, then here's some advice: stop reading at the end of this chapter, close the book, and pass it along to a friend who may also be considering freelancing. Granted, you spent a few hard-earned dollars to pay for this book, but your money wasn't wasted. After all, I did you one helluva favor. Think of all the agony and the struggles you might have endured if you *hadn't* read this chapter—if you had taken the freelance plunge without realizing the seas were quite so choppy.

As for those of you still interested in pursuing a freelancing career . . . well, hold onto your molars. This was only Round 1 in the Great Freelance Writing Reality Marathon. Round 2 gets a bit more personal as you examine what traits you'll need to cope adequately with this most unusual profession.

2 Assessing Yourself: Is Freelancing for You?

Each year, an unknown number of would-be writers decide they would like to become full-time freelancers. Some spend months in a futile effort to tally their first sale. Others manage to supplement a nonwriting income by selling an occasional magazine article. As for freelancing full time, the vast majority of "attemptees" simply never make it. In fact, most never should have tried. Very few people are cut out to become full-time freelance writers. Most simply are not suited emotionally, psychologically, or intellectually to handle such a career, regardless of whether or not they can actually write.

I can hear you now: *How arrogant! How patronizing! This guy sounds like he's trying to scare me just because he doesn't want any more competition. Who does he think he is, saying most people aren't qualified to do his job?*

By way of rebuttal, let me begin by saying I hope you *do* succeed and become a full-time freelance writer—if for no other reason than to satisfy my own ego. I'd love nothing more than to take at least partial credit for your success. If one day you wind up getting an assignment that would have otherwise gone to me, I can assure you I'd take such a "defeat" in stride. After all, it's hardly a loss when the pupil surpasses the teacher.

But it most definitely *is* a loss when someone embarks upon a career for which they plainly are not suited. True, you may have the *desire* to write. For that matter, you may also possess the *talent* to write. Yet to succeed professionally—to become a full-time freelance writer—you also must possess those personality traits which can translate your ambition and talent into reality.

In the previous chapter, I outlined the pros and cons of a career as a freelancer. Using that discussion as a background, this chapter explores freelancing on a more personal basis. How? By asking ten questions that should help you determine whether you've got what it takes to succeed as a freelancer.

Question 1: Are you one of life's gamblers or do you generally prefer to "play it safe"?

Opt for a career in business, medicine, or law and you stand a relatively good chance of achieving at least a modicum of success in those fields. After all, our society is always able to make room for one more executive, or doctor, or lawyer.

But should you decide to become a full-time freelance writer, the odds are definitely against you (only two- to three-hundred members in the club, remember?). True, there's always the possibility you'll achieve enormous success in the field. You could eventually wind up writing books, producing a string of lucrative, highly acclaimed best-sellers. Then again, even after five or ten years in the profession, you could find yourself with only a modest sales record, hefty debts, and growing doubts about the future.

Full-time freelancing is a gamble—much more of a gamble than most other professions. If you decide to pursue the profession, you must recognize that you *are* gambling and that the stakes are your own future. The rewards can be sizeable, but so are the risks.

So, if you're someone who prefers to play it safe, chances are that full-time freelancing is not for you. Stick to a less "iffy" career. And if you're one of life's gamblers, then do what any Las Vegas pro would do: assess the rewards *and* the risks before you decide to play.

Question 2: Do you work well in unstructured situations or are you the type of person who requires a great deal of supervision?

11

On paper, at least, being your own boss sounds ideal. Yet working for yourself means you'll be confronted continually by decisions affecting your career. For example, you'll have to decide what subjects to write about; how many assignments you can tackle at any given time; which magazines to query; which people you will need to interview; and where you should go to track down information.

If you're the type of person who relishes making decisions, you'll welcome the challenge of a freelancing career. But if you're indecisive by nature—if you would rather have someone else tell you what to do—then think again about becoming a full-time freelance writer. True, even successful writers sometimes make poor decisions. That's to be expected. But whether they turn out to be good or bad, established freelancers are not afraid to *make* decisions. What about you?

Question 3: Are you reasonably self-disciplined or would you rather have others exercise that discipline for you?

Being your own boss means you'll not only have to make your own decisions but that you'll also have to muster up a great deal of self-discipline. It's one thing to *decide* to write a particular article. It's quite another to *accomplish* that goal. Self-discipline is the mental muscle that translates your decisions into action. And the energy that fuels that muscle is motivation.

Basically, there are two types of motivation: external and internal. External motivation comes from supervisors, parents, spouses, friends—anyone other than ourselves. Internal motivation, on the other hand, is self-generated: it comes solely from within.

Hopefully, when you first begin your career as a freelancer, you'll be able to rely on others to provide you with a great deal of encouragement and moral support. But after a while, such outside motivation will wane. Even a concerned spouse often gets tired of providing day-to-day encouragement. In the long run, there's simply no substitute for self-motivation. The more you have, the easier it will be to exercise the self-discipline necessary for success in the field.

Question 4: Are you able to accept rejection in stride or are you particularly sensitive to rejection?

Unfortunately, rejection is an inevitable part of becoming a full-time freelance writer. In fact, it's not a question of *whether* you'll be rejected, but how frequently.

Most freelancers receive their rejection slips after they've queried a magazine with a suggestion for an article. If you've donned your emotional armor, you'll respond to such form letter rejections in a professional manner: you'll open the letter, shrug your shoulders, and dig out a copy of your original query. After retyping the query, you'll place it in an envelope and send it off to another magazine. If you're lucky enough to receive a personalized rejection containing some constructive criticism, all the better. If the criticism is valid, you can either rewrite your query to make it more effective or else you can aim your query at a different market. (We'll spend a whole chapter talking about queries later in the book.)

The worst thing you can do is to let rejection slips thwart your momentum, especially when you're just beginning in the profession. A rejection slip is not a no to Sandra Miller, the freelance writer; it's a no to Sandra Miller's *idea*. That's an important distinction. What's more, it's only *one* no. A single rejection—even several—doesn't necessarily mean that your idea is a bad one. There's always the chance that some editor—presumably, a wiser one—will eventually say yes and give your suggestion a go-ahead. But before that happens, you'll have to conquer your fear of rejection.

Question 5: Are you blessed with a great deal of persistence or do you tend to give up easily?

"Nothing in the world can take the place of persistence. Talent will not; nothing is more common than unsuccessful men with talent. Genius will not; unrewarded genius is almost a proverb. Education will not; the world is full of educated derelicts. Persistence and determination alone are omnipotent."

Although the press dubbed him "Silent Cal," President Coolidge was hardly mum when asked about the value of persistence. His words are particularly appropriate for aspiring freelancers because freelancing is one of the world's most discouraging professions. Rejections are common, progress is slow, and sales are sporadic. Few occupations require a greater degree of persistence. For despite all the disappointments and all the competition, you're going to have to keep trying, keep querying, keep thinking of new ideas, and most of all, keep writing if you want to succeed.

It's almost a certainty that the person with ten parts *persistence* but only five parts talent will outperform, outmarket, and outsell any writer who has ten parts *talent*, but only five parts persistence. If you're persistent by nature, you stand a reasonably good chance of succeeding at a full-time freelancing career. But if you're a quitter, if you often start projects but never complete them, if you give up when you confront the first obstacle, you might just as well forget about freelancing and pursue a less demanding profession.

Question 6: Are you assertive in your dealings with other people or do you consider yourself basically shy?

Shyness is a trait shared not only by would-be freelance writers but also by many business executives, athletes, and even Hollywood movie stars. In its most extreme form, shyness can hinder social development by preventing an individual from meeting new people or engaging in new experiences. Although relatively few cases are this severe, shyness remains an all-too-common affliction. After all, does *anyone* relish the idea of getting up before a large audience and speaking extemporaneously?

If you consider yourself shy, there's at least some good news in store for you: you don't have to be a skilled public speaker to become a full-time freelance writer. The bad news is that you will have to interact with strangers on a one-to-one basis. And *you're* the one who is going to have to initiate this interaction.

For example, let's suppose you're given the go-ahead to write an article on the danger that hurricanes pose to the residents of the Gulf Coast region. Quite obviously, you're going to need to talk with at least one meteorologist who specializes in hurricane forecasting. Unfortunately, no one's going to call you up on the phone and say, "Hi, I heard about the article you're working on, and since I'm an expert in the field, I thought you might need a little help. Now, what is it you need to know?"

If only it were that easy.

Instead, you're going to have to track down Mr. Hurricane Expert for yourself. You're going to have to begin by finding out who he is and where to reach him. Then you're going to have to call him and arrange an interview. Whether the interview takes place in person or over the phone, Mr. Hurricane Expert is not about to take the lead in the discussion. He has no idea what kind of information you're looking for. Regardless of the fact he's world-renowned, Mr. Hurricane Expert will expect *you* to take charge during the interview. So like it or not, you're going to have to be assertive. After all, you'll probably have to conduct several dozen—maybe a hundred or more—interviews each year.

Of course, this same assertiveness will be required when dealing with editors. If you're meek, passive, or docile, you risk being mistreated professionally. Then again, if you come on *too* strong— if you're arrogant, pushy, or abrasive—you risk alienating your editors and losing potential sales. The secret is to stand up for your rights without offending the person who is trying to trample them.

Remember, as a freelancer, you don't belong to a union or to a trade organization which represents you in disputes with "management." You're on your own. Unless you speak up for yourself, there's always the chance that some editor—whether intentionally or not—is going to treat you unfairly.

Question 7: Are you able to compromise or are you someone who prefers that things be done your way or not at all?

A few days after I turned in my very first magazine article to the editors of *Chicago*, I received a phone call. Would I mind stopping by the magazine's office to discuss my article? The call took me by surprise. What was there to discuss? I had been assigned to write a story about the feud between the air traffic controllers at O'Hare Airport and the FAA. I did my research and I wrote my article. Assignment complete. Finis.

Or so I thought.

Yet, during a brief meeting with one of *Chicago*'s editors, I discovered that things were far from finished. Instead, I was handed my original manuscript and asked to take it home, look it over, and approve the changes. Flipping through what was once a neat, clean, professional-looking manuscript, I was confronted with a blinding sea of blue pencil marks. Whole paragraphs had been deleted. Large question marks adorned several of the margins, and some paragraphs were shifted from one part of the manuscript to another. Although I kept my composure at the meeting, I was angry. Who did this editor think he was, messing around with *my* manuscript?

After two days of bemoaning the sorry state of American editing, I reread the much-altered manuscript and reached a startling conclusion: with few exceptions, Mr. Blue Pencil had substantially improved upon my original article. Admittedly, a few of my wordier—and to my mind, more poetic—passages had been deleted, but the result was a much tighter, better organized, and infinitely more interesting article.

I relate this story for a reason: no writer—not even the Mailers and Capotes—escapes the all-powerful blue pencil. In fact, that's one of the primary jobs of an editor: to edit. And editors usually are better at editing than writers. The reason? Because their egos are at stake, it is very difficult for writers to examine their work objectively. Instead, they have a tendency to look upon their prose as though the words were etched in stone. Beginning writers, especially, seem to suffer from this "read it, but don't change it" syndrome.

Still, good editing should be a team effort. After all, even the most competent editor cannot share the same perspective on an article as the writer who researched the piece. For this reason, most established freelancers are not hesitant about questioning changes in focus, content, quotations, and style, as well as a host of other variables. In most cases, a writer/editor compromise settles these minor differences of opinion.

The freelancer who is unyielding, who balks at being edited, or who ignores an editor's input, is not likely to maintain a career on a full-time basis. To be sure, there are times when a writer *should* be unyielding—for example, when an editor suggests fabricating quotations. But most writer/editor disputes involve mini-skirmishes, not major battles. Most can be solved harmoniously through compromise—as long as both parties are willing to practice some simple give-and-take.

Question 8: Are you a skeptic by nature or do you consider yourself a trusting individual?

If you decide to become a full-time freelance writer, sooner or later you'll probably write an article on a controversial subject. True believers, beware. For during the course of your interviews, you're going to encounter people who are going to tell you outright lies. Others will opt for half-truths, and still others will give you answers that are technically correct, but deceptive nonetheless.

As a responsible journalist, you have an obligation to your reader to expose the fiction and highlight the fact—not that "truth" is easy to discern. You're a writer, not a judge and jury. You don't have a hotline to heaven. Yet during your interviews, you're going to have to be at least modestly skeptical of what others tell you, particularly if the information could be considered at all self-serving.

This doesn't mean that you should automatically refuse to believe anyone who works for the federal government, Exxon, the National Rifle Association, or whatever organization you might happen to mistrust. But it does mean that when working on any article even remotely controversial, you must continually question the information you're given, rather than unhesitatingly accept it at face value. Who knows—as a healthy skeptic, you may just discover that it's not the public relations spokesman at the Pentagon who's been lying to you, but rather, that mild-mannered college professor who seemed as honest as your grand-dad.

Question 9: Can you accept a certain amount of financial insecurity or are you the kind of person who prefers to receive a regular paycheck?

Let's assume you work as a salesclerk in a department store, and you earn $15,000 a year. Every other Friday, your boss hands you a white envelope. Inside is your paycheck. Admittedly, your salary is hardly huge, and deductions such as taxes, health insurance, and Social Security payments eat away at your modest earnings. But at least you have a reasonably good idea of how much money you can expect to net. And at least you know *when* you'll receive your checks.

Now let's switch your career. This time you're a full-time freelance writer. Last year, you earned $20,000. But before you applaud your pay hike, consider this: that twenty grand didn't come neatly divided into twenty-six biweekly installments. Nor did anyone bother to deduct for taxes and Social Security. (You're your own boss, remember? That's *your* job.) Instead, you received thirty or forty different checks from a few dozen different publications, all of which had different payment rates. And because some magazines were more prompt than others in sending their payments, there were some months in which you received a few thousand dollars and others during which you didn't receive a penny.

And what about next year?

Well, if you're that department store salesclerk, you have a pretty good idea how much of a raise—if any—you're likely to receive. Add that to your present earnings, estimate your overtime pay, and your final prediction is likely to prove remarkably accurate.

If you're that freelance writer, on the other hand, you'll find the job of predicting next year's earnings well-nigh impossible. Ideally, your income will increase. At the very least, it should keep pace with inflation. But freelancing is a speculative occupation. It offers no guarantees, least of all financial ones. Reap a mini-windfall from your writing sales, spend it on something frivolous—but deserved—and you just might find yourself strapped for cash three months later when your sales hit a slump.

Of course, in this scenario at least, you *did* earn $5,000 more as a freeelance writer than as a salesclerk. But, in your opinion, does the possibility of earning a higher income—and it's only a possibility, not a guarantee—justify the financial uncertainty that comes with the profession? And how good are you at budgeting?

Not just budgeting from paycheck to paycheck, but long-range fiscal planning? For unless you boast a fat savings account or a Sugar Daddy with a fat wallet, you'll need to perform some pretty clever financial juggling in order to keep your fiscal head above water as a full-time freelancer.

Question 10: Do you have a good business sense or are you someone who loathes the idea of being a businessperson?

Writing may seem like one craft that transcends the oft-maligned world of ordinary business. Yet stripped of its literary pretensions, full-time freelance writing is, in many ways, just another business. And unless you treat it as such, your career is doomed to economic failure. Assuming you're not independently wealthy, you'll have to develop a good business sense if you want to earn a living at the profession. This means that eventually you're going to have to concern yourself with many of the same matters that confront the top executives at Boeing or General Motors: profits and losses, productivity measurements, cost-effective procedures, tax write-offs, and investment tax credits. Ideally, freelance writers shouldn't have to worry about such concerns. Yet if your long-range goal is to make a profit from your writing, then you'll have to start thinking like a businessperson.

So if the thought of managing such a business single-handedly is abhorrent to you—if you have a strong disdain for businesspeople and the business world—then perhaps you should reexamine your career goals. Otherwise you might wake up one morning, walk to the bathroom, and confront the "enemy" staring back at you in the mirror.

AND YOUR DECISION IS . . .

All right, it's decision time. Now you have to answer the most important question of all: is full-time freelance writing a career for which you are suited?

Before you answer, let me offer a suggestion. When you come to the end of this page, close the book and think about what you've read in these first two chapters. Mull it over. Talk about it with friends and family. Don't automatically assume that just because you've dreamed about becoming a freelancer for the last five years that the profession is ideal for you. (There is no "ideal" profession, remember?)

Reread the first chapter and go over the list of pros and cons again. Reevaluate your answers to the ten questions you just finished reading. Be honest with yourself. Sure, your sister's friend, Barry, has been a freeelancer now for nine years and loves it. But what about you? Freelancing may be right for Barry, but is it right for you?

If, after careful consideration, you decide you still want to become a full-time freelancer, then by all means, continue reading the book. Another fifteen chapters await you, providing step-by-step instructions and offering dozens of pointers on how to succeed in the profession.

But if you do decide to "take a pass" on pursuing the career, be philosophical. Applaud your decision, and begin setting your sights on another profession. And when you think back on your might-have-been career as a freelancer, remember this: no amount of wishful thinking could ever have transformed freelance writing into the glamorous occupation you envisioned it to be.

3 In Preparation for Your New Career....

If you've made it this far in your reading, you've obviously decided you're going to pursue a freelance writing career. Congratulations! You probably still have a few lingering doubts about your decision. That's to be expected. But you're also probably anxious to get started in your new profession.

Before you sit down and begin composing your first query letter, allow me to offer a potpourri of preparatory advice.

SUPPLY-SIDE WRITING

Back in Chapter 1, I mentioned that you would have to invest money in your freelancing career. Well, grab your checkbook and dig out your credit cards, because it's time to buy some office supplies.

What follows is a list of supplies you should consider purchasing before you begin to write. Due to inflation and regional price variations, no attempt has been made to quote prices. You can, however, often save considerable money on such purchases.

Whenever possible, buy stationery items in bulk quantities rather than individually. Granted, your original cash outlay will be greater. But the savings will accrue over the long run since the unit price is always lower on bulk orders.

Another tip: *make sure you save your receipts. You'll need them at tax time to verify your purchases.*

21

Armed with that advice, here's a suggested shopping list for the beginning freelancer.

A copy of WRITER'S MARKET. Published by the same firm that issues *Writer's Digest* magazine, *Writer's Market* is a freelancer's bible—and is nearly as sacred. This easy-to-use, 900-page reference book contains not only a carefully compiled listing of most U.S. magazines but also such useful information as article requirements, payment rates, and submission policies. Updated annually, *Writer's Market* is available in most bookstores.

Letterhead stationery. In one sense, a letterhead is an "essential nonessential." There's no rule of freelancing that says you *have* to use letterhead stationery. Editors will still read your correspondence if you type it on ordinary bond paper. But a letterhead is important because it tells an editor something about you— namely, that you're serious about your writing as opposed to being a "dabbler" in the craft. It says that the odds are fairly high that you're a professional (more on this subject later in the chapter).

To obtain your own letterhead stationery, contact any printer who does typesetting and ask to have 200 to 500 sheets printed on heavy white bond paper containing 25 percent rag. Avoid frills. Keep the format of your letterhead as simple as possible. After all, what you *write* should attract an editor's attention, not the flashy stationery on which you write it. Your best bet is to have your name centered and printed at the top of the page in capital letters. Insert an italicized "freelance writer" on the line below, and follow that by a line of smaller boldface type giving your street address, city, state, zip code, and phone number (include your area code).

Plain business-size (#10) envelopes (4 × 8 1/2 inches). Don't let your printer talk you into purchasing personalized envelopes, the kind that have your return address already embossed in the upper left-hand corner. They're a waste of money. Many editors don't even open their own mail, let alone examine envelopes.

Heavy white bond paper. Use this for typing your completed manuscripts. You can purchase a box of 500 sheets at any stationery store.

Plain typing paper. The cheaper the better, since you'll use it only for your rough drafts.

A box of carbon manifolds. These flimsy sheets of 8 1/2 × 11-inch paper will save you a fortune in photocopying costs. Attached to the front of each sheet is a piece of easy-to-remove carbon paper. When you're ready to type your final draft, just insert a carbon manifold behind a sheet of bond paper and presto—you automatically have a permanent copy for your files.

9 1/2 × 12 1/2-inch or 10 × 13-inch manila envelopes. You'll use them for mailing your manuscripts to editors.

Legal-sized pocket file folders. Assign one folder to each of your articles, and make sure every scrap of material pertaining to that article is stored in the proper folder.

A rubber stamp bearing your name and address. This one-time purchase will save you the hassle of typing your return address on all your correspondence. You can also put it to good use when preparing self-addressed envelopes. Check the Yellow Pages under "Rubber Stamps" for dealers in your area.

Postal scale. Before you send small packages through the mail, you'll need to weigh them so you can affix the proper postage. A wide variety of relatively inexpensive postal scales is available at most stationery stores.

A dictionary and a thesaurus. Paperback editions are easier to handle than bulky hardcover copies (something to consider, since you'll probably be consulting them fairly often).

Stamps—lots of them. In fact, you'll use so many, you might as well start buying rolls of a hundred instead of trudging off to the post office every few days. (Be sure to ask the clerk for a receipt—you won't get one otherwise.)

Business cards. Although you can easily get along without them in the beginning, eventually you'll want to return to the same printer who designed your letterhead and order a few hundred business cards. Most people you give them to will probably end up tossing them out, but you'll be able to make good use of them when you meet with editors and interviewees.

The design of your business card should be kept simple. Forget the maroon-colored card with a bright yellow stripe down the side and raised gold lettering. A plain, functional business card listing your name, occupation, address, and phone number is a much wiser investment than a card that screams "Notice me! Notice me!"

A typewriter. Although you may prefer to write your rough drafts in longhand, no editor will accept a handwritten query or manuscript. That's why you must have your own typewriter. Although you can probably get by for a few months by typing your final drafts on a friend's typewriter, in the long run, such an arrangement isn't very practical for you *or* your friend.

So if you don't already own one, you'll have to buy an electric typewriter—preferably an office model, but at the very least, a good electric portable. Editors *will* assign stories to writers who type their queries on manual typewriters, but no manual can ever give your final drafts the high-tech, professional appearance of an electric. The pros use electrics. So should you. (More on typewriters in Chapter 15.)

One last suggestion while we're on the subject: if you haven't already mastered the skill, learn how to type. In fact, start tomorrow. You don't have to enroll in a class, either. Find a friend who knows how to type and have him or her spend an hour or two teaching you the basics. Or get hold of a do-it-yourself book that will show you those basics in ten easy lessons. Learning isn't difficult. It's simply a matter of being shown where to place your fingers on the keyboard. The rest is practice—lots of it. Months from now, you'll probably agree that the old hunt-and-peck method—even your once-touted "high-speed" hunt-and-peck system—is no substitute for the two-hand, no-peeking technique used by the pros.

TIME TO WORK, TIME TO WRITE

How much time will you need to devote to your new career? Plenty. In fact, the more hours the better, especially when you're just beginning. But how do you find sufficient time to freelance when you also have to hold down a nonwriting job?

The most obvious answer is to quit your other job and devote all your energy to writing. That may be an obvious answer, but in most cases it's an impractical one, as well. After all, how are you going to pay your bills—from your writing? Well, your utilities, perhaps. But not your mortgage, your car loan, and your food bills—at least not in the beginning. The brutal fact remains that unless your savings account is brimming or your spouse is willing to support you, you're going to have to hold down a nonwriting job if you want to avoid starvation.

Certainly a nine-to-five office job will keep your pantry stocked and your landlady smiling. Provided you muster the self-discipline, you'll be able to tackle freelancing early in the morning, at night, and even on weekends. But though you may be able to *write* during such hours, researching and interviewing are another matter. Some libraries, for example, aren't open on Saturdays, let alone evenings. And as for conducting interviews, you'll find that many interviewees are nine-to-five folks themselves. Although most are usually more than happy to talk to you, they'd rather not be bothered at home. Instead, they expect to be interviewed at the office during—you guessed it—normal business hours.

Unfortunately, there is no easy solution to this "where do I find the time?" dilemma. But consider this: if you're dissatisfied with your present job and you're convinced it's not an occupation you want to puruse even if freelancing *doesn't* pan out, then you might think about taking temporary employment as a waiter/waitress, taxi driver, or bartender. Prestige jobs? Hardly. But what they lack in status, they can make up for by providing a steady income, one that's supplemented by tips. Best of all, such jobs don't lock you into the nine-to-five strait jacket. Instead, they can allow you to work at night, keeping your days free for writing.

Another advantage of accepting such stopgap employment is that you may have the option of reducing your working hours as your freelancing business increases. For example, when I first began writing, I worked at a restaurant five nights a week. Once my writing started to generate some modest revenue, I was able to reduce my restaurant schedule to just four nights a week, then three. During the time I waited on tables, my total income remained roughly the same. But gradually, I discovered I was earning a greater and greater *percentage* of my income from freelancing. Eventually, my writing proved profitable enough for me to say, "To hell with the waiter job," quit, and join the ranks of the full-time freelancers.

WRITING WELL, WRITING BETTER

Chances are, you can probably outwrite most of the people you know. In fact, you may already be a better literary craftsperson than even some established freelancers. But regardless of whether or not you possess a greater degree of raw talent, the freelancer with the track record still has a distinct advantage over you: he knows his genre of writing. What he may lack in style, he compensates for in form.

Ideally, your writing will reflect a skillful knowledge of both style *and* form. To succeed, however, you must possess more than a passing familiarity with the type of writing you're attempting to master. For this reason, I offer this suggestion: pay close attention to articles appearing in the top national publications. Study them. Analyze them. Dissect them. Play sleuth—try to discover why the article "works." Ask yourself why a magazine paid one thousand, two thousand, often three thousand dollars or more for those few pages of prose. You certainly don't want to mimic someone else's writing, but you should be curious about how your writing stacks up against that of the pros.

You also might want to go browsing through bookstores in search of how-to books on the art of writing. (I can offer you pointers on freelancing as a career, but I'm hardly qualified to teach you *how* to write.) Two excellent writing texts which I recommend highly are William Zinsser's book *On Writing Well* (Harper & Row) and Robert Morsberger's *Commonsense Grammar and Style* (Thomas Y. Crowell Company). Both are available in paperback.

THE AMATEUR VERSUS THE PRO

Letterhead stationery, business cards, and electric typewriters are standard tools of writing professionals. But professionalism is more than just a look or an appearance. It's also an attitude—the way in which an individual conducts his or her career.

Talk to any magazine editor in New York, and sooner or later you'll hear stories of very talented freelancers whose once-promising careers were cut short because of a lack of professionalism—not that they weren't good writers. It's just that they were unable to meet the professional demands of major league editors.

A professional is someone who performs his job in an efficient, businesslike manner. An amateur lacks such an approach. A professional writer agrees to a deadline, and does his best to ensure that a manuscript is on the editor's desk by that date. An amateur disregards deadlines, mails articles three weeks late, and never bothers to notify an editor of the delay. A professional submits a clean, legible manuscript. An amateur submits a sloppy manuscript riddled with errors and smudge marks. A professional is someone a magazine can rely upon to maintain a good image by conducting informative, productive interviews. An amateur brings discredit to publications by being tardy, unprepared, or rude.

In the long run, professionalism has nothing to do with the amount of time you've been writing. Some freelancers seem to be born with a professional attitude. Others could work at the craft for decades without ever rising above the rank of amateur. You can be sure that the people for whom you write and the people that you interview will know in an instant whether or not you're a pro. Editors prefer to give assignments to the pros. People who are being interviewed speak more candidly with professionals.

The letterheads, business cards, and fancy typewriters all help. But they're no substitute for that priceless and intangible quality: professionalism.

2 | THE PROFESSION OF FREELANCING

4 In Search of Article Ideas

A few years from now, your freelance career booming, you're going to be sitting in front of your typewriter, banging away at the keyboard, when suddenly the telephone rings. On the other end of the line is an editor, someone for whom you've written in the past and someone who's familiar with your work. Quite unexpectedly, this editor mentions that he's come up with a story idea. Then he pops the question. Are you interested in writing the article for the magazine? After catching your breath, you calmly agree to the request, knowing that this single phone call means you're probably a thousand dollars richer.

Such a scenario is hardly consigned to the realm of fiction. Editors make such requests all the time—at least to established freelancers. Not surprisingly, the ego boost is enormous. Here's an editor who has enough confidence in your abilities to assign you a story idea generated by the magazine itself.

IN THE BEGINNING, THERE WERE IDEAS

Since you're just beginning your career, you can't expect editors to come to you—not yet. Instead, you're going to have to approach the editors and suggest your *own* article ideas. All of which leads to one important question: What article ideas are you going to suggest?

You're going to have to answer that question before you sit

down to compose your first query letter. Somehow, some way, you're going to have to come up with a marketable idea that you can pitch to a magazine. And as soon as you've found it, you're going to have to think of another idea, and another, and another. The process never ends. Anyone hellbent on writing magazine articles has to generate dozens—even hundreds—of idea possibilities each year. There's simply no such thing as a freelancer with too many ideas.

How do you learn to develop story ideas? Where do such ideas originate?

Chances are you'll find at least some of your article ideas right in your own backyard.

INVOLVE YOUR INTERESTS, EXPLOIT YOUR EXPERTISE

One way to discover a wealth of article ideas is to ask yourself what subjects interest you. Are you an astronomy buff? A sports enthusiast? An opera fan? Whatever your areas of interest, use them as starting points for magazine article ideas. Ask yourself what kind of article *you* would like to see written about solar eclipses, the Super Bowl, or *Carmen*. Let your mind ponder the subject for a while. Read through any printed materials you might have and see if they trigger any ideas for articles. Visit the library and scan the *Reader's Guide to Periodical Literature* to discover what's been written on the subject in recent years. Who knows—you may find there's an obvious gap just waiting to be filled.

Your next step is to ask yourself what are the areas of human endeavor in which you excel. Nearly everyone is an expert of sorts at *something*. Certainly there's some field in which you possess greater knowledge than the average layman. What about a hobby? Do you repair autos in your spare time? Do you give piano lessons, or ski on weekends? If so, you may be able to come up with an idea for a "how-to" article. For example: "How to Avoid Auto Repair Ripoffs"; "How to Choose a Piano Instructor"; or "How to Avoid Skiing Injuries."

And what about your line of employment, either past or present?

Are you a registered nurse? A spokesperson for a trucking firm? An unemployed urban planner? Just about any job provides valuable "insider" information which can become the basis for a magazine article. Some examples: "What's Being Done to Prevent Nursing Burn-out?"; "The Case Against Trucking Deregulation"; or "The Role of the Auto in the Cities of Tomorrow."

Stated simply, the first rule for generating story ideas is, *Develop as many ideas as possible on subjects that interest you and subjects you know.*

Because you lack a track record of published articles, editors will be reluctant to give you your first assignment. Each would rather wait for some other editor to take that initial "gamble." (It's hardly your fault, but beginning freelancers don't have a very good reputation. Most lack a sense of professionalism.) When you're starting out, you're unable to cite recent articles of yours which have appeared in *Playboy, Parade,* or *People.* But you might be able to plug an article idea about airline flight oversales by boasting that you worked as an airline gate agent for four years at O'Hare. In fact, that's exactly how I obtained my first writing assignment from *ASTA Travel News.*

Remember: your first article will probably be the most difficult to sell. You certainly don't *have* to write your first piece on a familiar topic. But you're bound to improve your chances for a sale if you do. Besides, it's a lot easier to write about a subject you genuinely enjoy than one you despise.

YOU ARE WHAT YOU READ

Now that you've thought about tapping one of the most obvious sources of article ideas, you're ready for the next step in the Great Idea Search.

To find new ideas, read as many different publications as possible.

If your normal reading diet consists of nine parts fiction and one part fact, you might want to think about changing that ratio. In order to generate marketable ideas consistently, you'll have to stay abreast of current events. You'll need input on the developments of the day, and there's no better way to get this input than by reading nonfiction. After all, if this is what you'll be writing, it also should be what you're reading. So if you're not already a newsaholic, become one.

Start by religiously reading at least one newspaper a day, preferably more. Your local paper is a must. It can tip you off to a local story that has national implications, an angle that many editors prefer. One example is the story of a successful community anticrime patrol that is being monitored at the federal level.

If at all possible, you should also try to supplement your newspaper diet by regular reading of the *New York Times*, the *Washington Post*, or the *Los Angeles Times*. Generally considered to be the top thhree newspapers in the country, these papers provide comprehensive coverage of national and international developments. Most editors read at least one of these papers. If you don't live in New York, Washington, or Los Angeles, locate a bookstore or newsstand in your own community that sells out-of-town papers.

Whichever papers you read on a regular basis, make sure that you devour them from front to back. Don't limit your perusal only to the hard news stories, either. Read the business section, the entertainment pages, the gossip columns, the editorials—for that matter, even the obituaries. The more thorough your reading, the greater the likelihood is of spotting additional ideas for magazine articles.

ONE NEWSPAPER, TEN IDEAS

To illustrate this point, let's examine a single newspaper, the *Washington Post*, from October 9, 1981. Here are some possible subjects for magazine articles that I was able to glean from this one newspaper:

• A page-one story tells how a federal appeals court ruled against Arlington, Virginia's policy of strip-searching all suspects admitted to the county jail. During 1980, Arlington police strip-searched at least 4,500 suspects, even though some were charged only with petty offenses, such as playing their stereos too loudly. Although the article states that most communities permit such strip-searches only when suspects are admitted to jail for an extended period of time, it's clear that such a controversial policy remains on the books in at least some American communities.

Story idea: a survey article on the controversy surrounding strip-searches. Using Arlington as your lead, you could examine the pros and cons of such a hotly debated police procedure. (Arlington, for example, began strip-searching suspects after a shoplifting suspect with a revolver hidden in his pants leg fatally wounded a police officer.)

• Another front-page story deals with a proposal by the state of South Dakota to sell $1.4 billion worth of Missouri River water to a private energy developer for processing coal slurry. Said the *Post*, "The deal, which is being opposed by several downstream states, underscores a growing phenomenon in the Midwest and West in which the region's sparse water is becoming more valuable for the extraction and use of minerals than for farming and more traditional Western endeavors." In short, another classic progress/tradition confrontation.

Story idea: a detailed examination of the water wars raging in America's heartland. Another possibility: a story about how more and more states are locked in feuds which culminate in lawsuits. (Interstate air pollution is another example of this legal quagmire.)

• A photo on page two shows Mexico City's giant panda frolicking with her newborn cub, "only the second giant panda to be naturally conceived and born in captivity."

Story idea: an article describing the difficulties faced by zoo officials in getting pandas to mate in captivity.

• On page thirteen, the *Post* carries a story about how U.S. government scientists in California suspect that increases in radon gas may be a warning of an impending earthquake in Southern California.

Story idea: an examination of the latest advances in the iffy science of earthquake prediction. Another possibility: assuming the science of earthquake prediction *is* perfected, how will local governments use such warnings to save lives? Or will they be reluctant to broadcast warnings for fear of causing severe economic or social disruption?

• An editorial dubbed "Snake Eyes" argues that Congress (which still oversees Washington, D.C., affairs) should not overrule the city's attempt to introduce legalized gambling.

Story idea: plagued by budgetary woes, are more and more cities turning to gambling as a means of increasing revenues? How successful are state- and city-sponsored gambling programs? What are the tradeoffs?

• The obituary section recounts the death of a Maryland advertising executive who died when the biplane he was piloting crashed into a schoolyard. According to the *Post*, the plane's propellor flew off in flight.

Story idea: What steps can private pilots take to ensure better maintenance of their aircraft?

Other items in the same edition of the *Post* suggest even more article ideas:

• A short news blurb in the local section tells how a D.C. taxi driver was barred from picking up fares at Washington National Airport because he repeatedly overcharged his customers.

• A "Style" section article describes local roommate referral services.

• An article in the business section focuses on a CBS/AT&T plan for a two-way home information system for consumers.

• The feature story in the "Weekend" section tells why collectors are willing to pay high prices for vintage postcards.

By compiling this list, I'm not suggesting the *Washington Post* as the sole source of article ideas. Hardly. Nearly any edition of any big-city paper contains the seeds of several ideas. The point is that you're going to have to change the way you *read* a newspaper—any paper—if you're searching for story ideas. Admittedly, you may have to practice a bit before you can come up with ten ideas from one paper, but after a while, you'll find that idea hunting not only becomes easier and easier, but also more profitable.

Looking back on my own career, I can recall numerous examples when newspaper stories led to actual sales.

THE $500 CLIPPING

On June 25, 1975, I walked to the corner newsstand and paid 15 cents for a copy of the *Chicago Daily News* (an evening paper that has since expired). Upon returning home, I plopped myself down in a lawn chair and began reading. I soon came across an article entitled "O'Hare Controllers Sue the FAA." The subtitle read "Job conditions threaten air safety." Having worked at O'Hare, I found the subject intriguing. Who knows, I thought. Maybe this could be the basis for a magazine article.

After thinking about the *Daily News* clipping for a few weeks, I finally decided that the FAA/controller feud would make an ideal topic for an article. So I queried the editor of *Chicago* magazine with the suggestion and waited patiently for a response. Much to my delight, the magazine was receptive to my idea and, after meeting with the editor, I received the go-ahead to write the piece. Entitled "Torment in the Tower," the article was published in the April 1976 issue of the magazine.

Had I not read the *Daily News* that June afternoon, there may never have been a story on air controllers in *Chicago*. But as it turned out, my 15-cent investment in a daily newspaper earned me a $500 check and my very first sale.

Newspapers have provided me with other story ideas:

● A 1979 op-ed piece in the *Washington Post* argued that instead of locking up nonviolent offenders in overcrowded prisons and jails, they should be sentenced to restitution and/or community service programs. That idea made so much sense to me that I pitched the suggestion to *Reader's Digest*. The resulting article, "Criminal Punishment that Pays Off," appeared in the magazine's July 1980 issue.

● A July 29, 1976, article in the *Chicago Daily News* was headlined "Want a Longer Life? Raise a Fuss, Prof Advises." The piece told of a Minnesota psychologist who had isolated five traits common to people who live a long life. That newspaper clipping provided the basis for a story on longevity that I sold to *Glamour*.

● A full-page profile of a University of Chicago tornado expert in the *Chicago Tribune* led to an article on tornado research for *Science Digest*.

THERE'S GOLD IN THEM THAR PUBLICATIONS

Newspapers probably provide the greatest single source of magazine articles for most full-time freelancers, but other publications can also work wonders in triggering a writer's brain cells. Among them:

MAGAZINES
Back in 1978, I was flipping through the "Frontlines" section of *Mother Jones* when I spotted a three-paragraph item entitled "London Buses." The story mentioned how the English double-deckers were being used in Davis, California, as part of that city's effort to implement its own, far-reaching energy conservation program. As it turned out, that *Mother Jones* clipping provided the basis for another *Reader's Digest* article, this one entitled "Where Energy Conservation Is a Way of Life."

Often, one magazine article can breed another. A case in point: an article on U.S. political assassinations that appeared in a 1976 issue of *Playboy*. My curiosity was piqued by a single paragraph in that article, in which the author told how several key witnesses to the J.F.K. assassination had met violent deaths within a few years after the president was slain. That lone paragraph prompted some extensive research, and the result was a March 1977 article that I wrote for *Argosy* entitled "The Bizarre Deaths Following J.F.K.'s Murder."

ENCYCLOPEDIAS, ALMANACS, AND REFERENCE BOOKS
Even the most seemingly mundane reading materials can provide article ideas. For example, one day while browsing through a section of the *Information Please Almanac* labeled "Disasters," I stumbled upon a fascinating discovery: between 1954 and 1969, five devastating fires occurred aboard U.S. aircraft carriers, all of them involving a significant loss of life. This information provided the basis for an article called "Flattop Fires" that appeared in—where else?—*Firehouse* magazine.

NEWSLETTERS
For several years, I subscribed to the *U.S. News & World Report Washington Letter*. In the spring of 1978, I spotted a short item that told how earth-sheltered homes and offices were one answer to soaring utility costs. The idea appealed to me, and I eventually wrote a magazine article on underground architecture which ap-

peared in the February 1979 issue of *Smithsonian*. Largely as a result of that article, I later signed a contract with E. P. Dutton to write my first book, *Earth Shelters*, which was published in September 1981.

LOOK, LISTEN, AND ASK QUESTIONS

By this time, you probably have a pretty good feel for how newspapers, magazines, and other publications can generate article ideas. A note of caution, however, should be sounded here. In your never-ending search for ideas, don't neglect the everyday events of life. Whether you're chatting away at a cocktail party, inching your Datsun through rush-hour traffic, shouting your lungs out at a football game, or frantically scurrying to complete your last-minute Christmas shopping, you'll find there are ideas all around you—*provided you're curious.*

For example, you overhear one of the guests at the cocktail party say that he recently purchased a "time-share" in a Hawaii condominium. What does such an arrangement involve and is it catching on?

You're sitting at a red light when you glance in your rearview mirror and notice an ambulance threading its way through the rush-hour tie-up. What kinds of problems does traffic congestion pose for emergency vehicles such as ambulances, police squad cars, and fire trucks?

After being tackled on the twenty-yard line, the quarterback is removed from the game with a severe knee injury. Why is the knee so susceptible to injury, and what precautions—if any—can "weekend athletes" take to prevent such injuries?

While waiting for an elevator in a department store, you spot a security guard apprehending a shoplifter who has set off an electronic alarm. What types of sophisticated electronic gadgetry are now being used in the war on shoplifters?

JOT IT DOWN, CLIP IT OUT

To prevent those money-earning ideas from simply vanishing into thin air, remember this advice.

39

Whenever you think of an article idea, jot it down as quickly as you can. It's a good idea to carry a pen and a small note pad with you at all times. When you discover an item in a newspaper or magazine that triggers an idea, cut it out immediately, date it, and save the clipping. I keep a single-edge razor blade in my office and use it to remove clippings for my files. Another suggestion is to take one of those manila file folders and label it "Ideas." This way you know exactly where to look for all your clippings. Rest assured, they'll come in very handy when you're composing your queries and getting started on your research.

Of course, not all of your ideas are going to pan out. You can't expect them to. For a variety of reasons, which we'll discuss later, many ideas simply never make it past the conceptualization stage. Still, ideas are the first step toward achieving your first sale. The next step is trying to find an editor to thinks your ideas are as great as you do.

5 Article Marketing 101

By this time, you've probably thought of several ideas that would make good subjects for magazine articles. Before you begin thinking about which magazines to query, you should examine your ideas to make sure they're marketable in their present form. Because unless they *are* marketable, you'll just be wasting your time trying to pitch them to editors. Your queries will be doomed before you even drop them in the mailbox.

FOCUS, ANGLE, TIMELINESS

One way to ensure the marketability of your ideas is to tighten the focus of your suggestions. Consider the subject of nutrition, for example. In the last few years, there have been hundreds of articles written on the subject for U.S. magazines. Even so, that doesn't mean an editor will automatically say no thanks if you, too, suggest an article on nutrition.

But you'll virtually be assured of getting such a rejection if you write a query that basically says, "Would you be interested in a story on the benefits of good nutrition?" Such a suggestion lacks focus. It's too broad, too general. Worst of all, it sounds boring as hell.

But a nutrition story can elicit a go-ahead *if* it's properly focused. Consider such ideas as "How California Schools Are Teaching Children Good Nutrition Habits"; "Diet and Baldness: Is There a Link?"; or "The Ten Most Common Myths About Good Nutrition." Although all three of these suggestions deal with the same topic, the scope of each idea has been narrowed considerably. Instead of looking at good nutrition as a whole, the focus has been refined to zero in on individual aspects of good nutrition.

Giving your story an "angle" will also improve its marketability. Basically, an angle is a different way of looking at a common subject—a new twist to a familiar theme. Readers love articles that have an interesting angle—so, for that matter, do editors.

Let's say, for example, that you want to write a story about the latest methods used to nab shoplifters. Focusing on state-of-the-art electronic gadgetry is one way to approach the story. But what about an article describing how ex-shoplifters in Houston have teamed up with the police to foil their former accomplices in crime? Now *that's* an angle.

Or suppose you want to write about the link between films and violence. As it stands, the subject is too broad. You need a focus and an angle. Then one day, you read a short newspaper item about a Chicago psychiatrist who maintains that twenty-five Americans shot themselves to death after watching the Russian roulette scenes in the movie *The Deer Hunter*. Suddenly, you discover your angle: "The Movie That Kills Its Viewers."

And then there's the matter of timeliness. Ordinarily, a story idea on the general subject of comets would be too broad to pique the interest of most editors. But you can bet your bookmark that in 1986, the year Halley's Comet returns to brush by the earth, you'll be reading all sorts of comet stories in all sorts of magazines. In 1986, comets will be a timely topic.

Several of my own articles were published primarily because they dealt with timely subjects. For example, following Betty Ford's admission that she was addicted to alcohol and prescription drugs, I wrote a piece for *Glamour* entitled "What You Should Know About Tranquilizers." After the Saudis suggested the idea of using icebergs as a source of fresh water, I wrote a story for *Science Digest* called "Big Eye on Icebergs." And when the gas lines began forming again in 1979, I was able to pitch a mass transit story to *Parade* called "Out of Gas? Take a Trolley."

To recapitulate, sharp focus, a clever angle, or a timely suggestion will greatly enhance the marketability of your ideas.

Keeping this maxim in mind, go over your own ideas once again and see what you can do to improve their marketability. If you still want to write a story about subways, but you haven't narrowed the focus, developed a unique angle, or thought of a timely peg, then put the idea on hold for a while. For now, just take one of those manila file folders and label it "Subways." Every time you come across another printed item on the subject, just toss it in the file. Sometime in the future, you might be flipping through the file and discover a marketable idea, one which eludes you today.

HOW TO USE THE FREELANCERS' BIBLE

Assuming each of your ideas now passes the marketability test, it's time to try to marry your ideas to the right magazines.

Let's assume, for a moment, that you have an article idea that was first triggered by the growing alligator population in your home state of Louisiana. It seems that not too long ago, the government established stiff penalties to protect from poachers what was then an endangered species. But the law has worked so well that now alligators are crawling into backyard swimming pools, scaring the neighbors out of their wits.

Wisely, you've decided you're not going to suggest an article entitled "Everything You Always Wanted to Know About Alligators." Instead, your tentative title is "Endangered Species That Are Out of Danger." In the article, you plan to argue that as a result of endangered species laws, many animals—including the alligators in the Bayou—are no longer in danger of extinction. In short, a "Man Helps Mother Nature" success story.

Temporarily, you set this idea aside and reach for your trusty copy of *Writer's Market*. Glancing through the table of contents, you notice that the two longest sections are entitled "Consumer

Publications" and "Trade, Technical, and Professional Journals." Little wonder that *Writer's Market* is such an indispensable tool, especially for the beginning freelancer.

In order to obtain capsule profiles of each publication, the editors of *Writer's Market* send questionnaires to the various magazines. When flipping through the book, you'll notice that some listings are much longer than others. That doesn't mean that *WM*'s editors are trying to plug any particular publications. They're not. It means only that some magazines took the time to respond to all of the items in the *WM* questionnaire, while others did not.

Writer's Market would be worth its purchase price if it did nothing more than simply list the names, addresses, and editors of the nation's magazines. But it does far more than that. In most cases, it provides a detailed description of each magazine. Make it a habit to read a magazine's entire description, and pay particularly close attention to the following information.

The description of the magazine's readership. Is the magazine aimed at Methodist teenagers, prospective buyers of high-fidelity components, or a general readership? In short, how sophisticated is the magazine's audience? And how qualified are you to write for that audience?

The number of freelance articles puchased annually. Not all the magazines provide this information in their *WM* listing. But it's obvious that you're far better off querying a magazine that buys a hundred articles a year rather than querying one which buys only eight.

Payment on acceptance or publication. A vital piece of information if there ever was one. Payment on acceptance means that once your editor has approved your manuscript, you can usually expect a check in the mail anywhere from one to five weeks later. Nearly all the top magazines have a "payment on acceptance" policy.

Unfortunately, an appalling number of magazines will not pay a writer until the article has been published. Freelancers find this policy offensive (to say the least) because magazines are notorious for waiting months, sometimes even a year or more, before they publish accepted manuscripts. And the longer it takes for your article to appear in print, the longer it takes for you to get paid. Never mind that no self-respecting editor would ever dream of telling a sporting goods clerk that since it's only July, he'd rather not pay for his skis until he uses them in February. Some editors have no qualms about withholding your payment until they get around to publishing your article.

But when you're just starting out, it will be hard for you to avoid the "payment on publication" magazines. During my first two years of freelancing, I wound up writing for several of these magazines, always rationalizing my decision with the argument, "At least it's a sale. Besides, I need the credit." As my career progressed, however, I eventually declared war on the pay-on-publication mongers, vowing to write only for magazines that paid on acceptance. As it turned out, I broke my vow twice— the first time with *Smithsonian* (an excellent magazine which should know better), and the second time with *Parade* (which has a neither-here-nor-there policy called "payment upon assigning the article for publication"—whatever that means). Reluctantly, I decided to back off from my oath because *Smithsonian* and *Parade* are such excellent credits.

Nonfiction needs. This is where the various editors speak directly to freelancers, outlining exactly what kinds of articles they're seeking. Pay close attention to what they have to say and note what they're willing to pay. And by all means, take the editors at their word. If they say "no how-to articles," that's exactly what they mean. If they say they must have photos with their stories, it won't do you any good to write a query unless you're certain you can get hold of the necessary pictures. (More on this subject in Chapter 8.)

In order to better familiarize yourself with *Writer's Market*, spend a few hours browsing leisurely through the various magazine listings. Read the listings carefully. Also, pay close attention to subheadings which have particular appeal to you. For example, if you're a sports car buff, be sure to look at the section entitled "Automotive and Motorcycle." If you enjoy dabbling in chemistry and physics, check out the "Science" section. And also consult the more generalized sections, such as "General Interest," "Men's," "Women's," "In-Flight," "Regional," "City," and "Newspapers and Weekly Magazine Sections."

THINK SMALL, BUT NOT TOO SMALL

Using the listings in *Writer's Market* as our guide, let's try to find a magazine that might be receptive to your endangered species story.

Flipping through the "General Interest" section you come across a familiar publication: *National Geographic*. Suddenly, you can envision your article all laid out in type, beautifully illustrated with breathtaking color photos, your by-line printed boldly beneath the title.

"Eureka!" you shout. "That's it. The endangered species story is *perfect* for *National Geographic!*"

Well . . . yes and no. Let me explain.

At the risk of second-guessing the magazine's editors, *National Geographic* might, just might, find such a story idea appealing. Yet even if the *Geographic* editors *love* your idea, they're not likely to assign *you* the story. The reason: you're an unknown. You have to establish yourself as a professional freelancer.

Keep in mind that because the magazine pays so well—often $4,000 or more for a single article—some of the top freelancers in the country are vying for its limited editorial space. These are the pros, the people who have already established a proven track record of performance. Not surprisingly, they're the kind of writers with whom the *Geographic* and other top magazines prefer to work.

Of course, nothing's impossible. You could sell your very first article to *National Geographic*. There's just one catch: you'd have to offer a pretty spectacular article—say, a first-person account of a hike up Everest—before the editors would give you an assignment. For this reason, you might as well forget about selling your first magazine article to a top-of-the-line publication such as *National Geographic*.

Basically, the same holds true for other top national publications. With very few exceptions, such magazines will probably reject your queries outright. Since they pay a lot, they expect a lot. And right or wrong, they think they're better off sticking with pros than gambling on beginners. Eventually, of course, if you're good, you'll crack the top markets. You'll have to if you want to make a living at the profession. But now is *not* the time to go querying *Playboy, McCall's* or *Reader's Digest.* You'll be receiving enough rejection slips as it is. There's no sense in courting more.

Okay, you say. Then what about *Bird Watcher's Digest,* which is listed in the "Nature, Conservation, and Ecology" section? You could slant the story so it focuses on successful programs to preserve endangered birdlife.

Good idea, except for one problem: *Bird Watcher's Digest* only pays $50 for a story. Now you're aiming your sights too low.

Think of the nation's magazines as forming a pyramid. At the top of this pyramid are the "biggies," the best national publications, which pay $1,000 or more for each story. Toward the upper third of the pyramid are the middle-level publications, paying anywhere from one hundred to several hundred dollars per story. And at the bottom of this pyramid are the countless small publications ($100 or less), many of which pay as little as a penny or two a word. (To get some idea what a pittance this truly is, consider this: if *Reader's Digest* paid just a penny a word for their articles, the average writer would earn just $15!) Some magazines are so strapped for cash, they don't pay *at all.* In lieu of money, they agree to send you a copy of the magazine once your article is published. Lucky you!

AIM FOR THE MIDDLE

As a general rule, my advice is to forget about these lower-level publications. (This advice is based on economics, nothing more. No slight is intended toward *Bird Watcher's Digest* or any other small magazine.) No doubt you're anxious to see your name in print—and earn a credit. That's understandable. But why write for a magazine that won't pay you what your article is truly worth? (Unless, of course, you can afford to subsidize your first few articles.) Besides, there *is* an alternative.

When you're starting out, focus most of your attention on

those magazines in the middle-level category, especially the ones paying $100 to $400 per story.

Granted, $100 is not a great deal of money for an article that may take two weeks or more to research and write. But you have to get your feet wet and establish your credentials as a professional beforee you can expect larger payments. That's why you should target these middle-level magazines. Once your articles appear in such publications, you can begin raising the eyebrows of other editors who pay a great deal more.

Keeping this "aim for the middle" suggestion in mind, go back through *Writer's Market* and carefully reread the listings. Whenever you find a magazine which qualifies for this middle-level designation, place a red check mark beside the entry so it will be easier to spot when you browse through the book later. Give the magazine two check marks if it also pays on acceptance. Reread the editorial needs of these publications, keeping in mind the kind of audience for which each is written. With enough searching, you'll probably find at least one, and possibly several magazines which would be likely candidates for each of your article ideas.

Then, too, you can always turn the tables around and put the marketing cart before the idea horse. In other words, if you spot a magazine you'd like to write for, carefully read the editorial needs of that publication and *then* sit down to think of an idea.

Now let's go back to the endangered species story. Under the heading "Nature, Conservation, and Ecology," you'll notice there's also an entry for *National Parks & Conservation Magazine*. Because it pays $75 to $200 for articles, *NP&C* seems to qualify as a medium-level publication. The magazine also pays on acceptance—two red check marks. And since *NP&C* is looking for articles dealing with "wildlife problems and wildlife appreciation," the magazine sounds as though it might be interested in your endangered species idea. The only potential drawback is that *NP&C* asks freelancers to state the availability of photos when they query.

KNOW YOUR TARGETS

Before you sit down to write your query to *National Parks & Conservation Magazine*, you would be smart if you did a bit of homework. For unless you're an avid conservation/ecology buff, you've probably never heard of *NP&C*, much less glanced through an issue of the magazine. True, *NP&C* editors provide a brief description of their publication in *Writer's Market*. But if your goal is to earn a go-ahead, you'll want to know as much about the magazine as possible.

Before you query, always examine back issues of the magazine to familiarize yourself with the content, style, and editorial focus of the publication.

Visit your local library and thumb through back copies of the magazine. Because *NP&C* is a special-interest magazine, it's unlikely you'll find copies available at branch libraries. Instead, head for the main library downtown and visit the periodical reading room.

An alternate suggestion is to write the magazine and request a sample copy. You'll notice that some of the magazine listings in *Writer's Market* say "Free sample copy." To take advantage of that offer, just request a copy on your letterhead stationery. In the case of *NP&C*, the *Writer's Market* listing indicates there is a $2 charge for a sample copy, so be sure to enclose a check with your request.

In the same letter in which you request a sample issue, you should also ask the magazine to send you a copy of their writer's guidelines. These are generally one or two-page photocopied sheets which provide an outline of the magazine's editorial needs, usually more detailed than what you'll find in *Writer's Market*. Such guidelines are almost always free, although you should enclose a self-addressed stamped envelope (SASE) with your request.

IN PREPARATION FOR YOUR QUERY

Now, a few suggestions before you sit down to compose your query letter. First, while you're at the library, glance through recent issues of the *Reader's Guide to Periodical Literature* to see whether a story idea like yours has already been published, and if so, where. With the endangered species idea for example, you may learn that *NP&C* recently printed a similar article on the subject. If that's the case, you'll have to go back to *Writer's Market* and find another prospect for your idea.

Second, be sure to check out the updated market listings which appear monthly in *Writer's Digest* magazine. (*The Writer* also carries such updates, but they're not as extensive as those in *WD*.) Who knows—you just might find that a new magazine, *Wildlife Forever*, has appeared on the market and is anxious to hear from freelancers.

Lastly, the endangered species idea is merely an example, which I've used to illustrate the secrets of good marketing. Don't— I repeat, *don't*—send the editors of *National Parks & Conservation Magazine* that suggestion. By this time, they've probably run more than one piece on the subject, and I'll never hear the end of it if they start receiving ten proposals a week entitled "Endangered Species That Are Out of Danger."

Besides, by this time, you should have plenty of your own ideas, as well as a pretty good idea of which magazines you're going to query. Now it's time to head for the typewriter to start cranking out those proposals.

6 The All-Important Query

Query. It's a word that has been popping up continually ever since you began reading this book. By now, you're probably saying to yourself, "What's all this talk about queries? Why not just write the article, send it in, and see whether or not an editor likes it?"

Good question. Now for some good answers.

To begin with, most editors prefer receiving queries rather than unsolicited manuscripts. If you want to verify the truth of that statement, just check the magazine listings in *Writer's Market*. In entry after entry, you'll find the same admonition: query first. From an editor's standpoint, the advice makes sense. Editors are busy people. They'd much rather say yea or nay to a one-page query than spend their time wading through an entire manuscript, which may turn out to be unsuitable for the magazine.

Queries save a lot of time, not only for editors, but for freelancers as well. Once you get the hang of it, you'll probably be able to compose a query in just a couple of hours. Obviously, there's no way you could both research and write an entire article in just two hours. Also, why bother to write the article if no editor is interested in it? The purpose of a query is to see what kind of a response your idea elicits from editors. If you're given a go-ahead, great! Start your research, write the article, and send it in. And if you can't find a single editor who likes your story idea, at least you haven't written an entire manuscript for naught.

Unless a Writer's Market *listing specifically states "Send completed manuscript only," always query a magazine before you begin writing an article.*

FIRST IMPRESSIONS

Pretend, for a moment, you're an aspiring ballet star. Ever since you were a child, you've been dreaming about dancing the lead in *Swan Lake.* You know you have the talent. You certainly have the ambition. All you need is that lucky break.

That break arrives when a friend wangles an audition for you with the artistic director of a world-famous ballet troupe. Unfortunately, your audition quickly turns into a fiasco. To begin with, you arrive looking like a mess. Your hair is uncombed, your appearance is haggard, and even your tutu looks tattered. When introduced to the artistic director, you mispronounce the man's name and begin babbling an embarrassing chorus of inanities. Worse, when asked to perform, you stumble all over yourself, unsure of exactly what you're doing. And little wonder. You didn't even take the time to rehearse for your audition.

In short, you were totally unprofessional. As a result, you made one helluva poor impression. Never mind that you might possess infinitely more dancing skills than the performers already in the troupe. You had your chance and you blew it. There's no way this artistic director will ever permit *you* to perform for *his* company.

What does this little sketch have to do with querying? Plenty. For in the world of freelance writing, a query is the literary equivalent of an audition. It's an opportunity for you to put your best foot forward—a chance to razzle-dazzle an editor not only with a good idea, but with your writing prowess as well. Granted, you might never meet this editor face-to-face. But rest assured he'll be able to tell a great deal about you from your query.

For no matter how intriguing your idea, no matter how perfect it might seem for a particular magazine, a poorly *presented* query will net you a rejection, not a go-ahead. However, a concise, well-written, well-thought-out, and provocative query can earn your idea star billing in the magazine's table of contents. Certainly you, as a freelancer, have a decided advantage over the aspiring dancer. When auditioning in front of an artistic director, a dancer only has one chance to make a good impression. A freelancer, on the other hand, can take hours, even days composing a single query, revising and perfecting that query until it's a work of art—which is precisely what it *should* be before you drop it in the mail.

Queries, then, are serious business. They can make or break your career. The more care you give to writing your queries, the greater the likelihood you'll be able to quit your other job and join the ranks of the full-time freelancers.

THE PREQUERY CHECKLIST

Before an airline flight even departs from the gate, the cockpit crew conducts a preflight check to make sure that all of the plane's systems are functioning properly. You should do the same thing with your queries. Before you start to write any query, you should ask yourself the following questions:

Is this an idea that truly interests me? Once, during the course of my own career, I queried several magazines with an idea about the growth of hospices, places where terminally ill patients can spend the last few weeks or months of their lives. The idea sounded as though it had story possibilities, especially since the subject hadn't received much press coverage. I never wrote the article because my query failed to trigger any go-aheads. Thank God. Because now that I look back on it, I really wouldn't have enjoyed researching and writing an article on hospices. The subject is a valid one, to be sure. But for me, anyway, it would have been a depressing subject to write about.

What about your own ideas? Are you really excited about them? At this point, no doubt, you're anxious for *any* sale, even if the article deals with a subject that's not all that appealing to you. But the more interested you are in the topic, the easier it will be for you to write the article. And the easier it is to write, the greater the chance it will be purchased and published.

Is this the right magazine to query? Presumably your idea passes the focus/angle/timeliness test. But from what you've gleaned from *Writer's Market* and from what you've learned by flipping through back issues of the magazine, is this idea suitable for this particular market?

Obviously, there's no way for you to be certain of the answer until you send your query and receive a response. At the same time, you should avoid a "shotgun" approach to querying. Too often, freelancers have a tendency to think, "According to *Writer's Market*, this magazine probably won't be interested in my idea. But what the hell? I'll send it anyway. All they can do is say no." True. But an editor just might remember your name the *next* time you mail in a query and dismiss your idea without reading it, simply because you were so off-target the first time.

Still, if you have an honest doubt as to whether a magazine will be interested in your idea—and such doubts are bound to crop up—then by all means, mail the query. Shortly after I wrote my first article for *Chicago*, I learned of a psychiatrist's proposal to help O'Hare controllers deal with the stress generated by their jobs. Good idea for another article, I thought. And sure enough, while flipping through *Writer's Market*, I came across the listing for *Psychology Today*. Yet although *PT* seemed like a likely candidate for my idea, I was skeptical about querying the magazine, because most authors in *Psychology Today* are—surprise!—psychologists and psychiatrists. What chance did I, an ordinary layman, have to write for such a magazine?

As it turned out, I put aside my doubts and sent the query. To my amazement, the response was positive; I received a go-ahead and wrote the story. The resulting article, "Sweaty Palms in the Control Tower," appeared in the February 1977 issue of *Psychology Today*.

The moral: when in doubt, query.

Do I have enough facts to compose my query? In order to generate a go-ahead, a good query has to contain enough facts, enough hard information, to prove there is a bona fide story behind the idea. Take the endangered species story, for example. It's not enough for your query to mention how alligators in Louisiana are now breeding like rabbits, thanks to the thoughtfulness of Man. You should also provide a brief history of the endangered species legislation (perhaps a sentence or two), the original controversy surrounding that legislation, as well as the result of such legislation (namely, that alligators and other animals are now thriving, where once they were imperiled).

How do you locate such information? Well, you have to do a little research, a subject we'll explore more thoroughly in Chapter 8. Granted, your query research doesn't have to be as thorough as when you write a complete article. But unless your query presents enough facts, you risk sabotaging what might otherwise be a highly saleable idea.

How difficult will it be for me to research the article if I eventually do get the go-ahead? Suppose you want to write a query suggesting an article on a possible breakthrough in cancer research. It seems that a team of Italian doctors is having amazing success curing cancer of the lymph nodes. Good idea. But how are you going to research such an article if you get a go-ahead? Fly to Rome to interview the Italian physicians? Conduct long-distance interviews over the phone with the help of an interpreter? Wade through the latest Italian medical journals?

Admittedly, this is an extreme example. No editor in his right mind would assign you such a story unless you were able to convince him you could adquately conduct the research. Every article requires research, and for this reason, you should be reasonably certain that you'll be able to uncover the facts necessary to write your article.

Is this query properly timed? In the last chapter, I mentioned the iceberg story which I sold to *Science Digest*. Imagine, for a moment, that you're an editor and that you're thinking about running such an article in your magazine. When would you schedule that story? For the July or August issue? Hardly. Think of icebergs and you think of winter, not summer. So the most likely time for an iceberg story to appear in print is between December and February.

Now, when should you query an editor with that story? In the middle of winter, right? Wrong. A monthly magazine like *Science Digest* has a long "lead time." In other words, right now the staff of the magazine is probably putting together an issue that won't appear on the newsstands for another three months, maybe longer. That's why I queried *Science Digest* in mid-August with the suggestion for the iceberg piece. It was a chilly proposal for a warm summer's day—but it earned me another by-line the following January.

It's important to think about lead times when you're submitting seasonal stories. If your story has a Christmas peg, for example, begin querying in July (assuming your target is a monthly magazine). Better to send your proposal too early than too late. If necessary, you can put your idea on hold for a few months. You're far better off waiting until your timing is right rather than courting an almost sure rejection when your timing is wrong.

THE SECRETS OF WRITING A GOOD QUERY

During my career as a freelancer, I've written hundreds of queries. Three of the better ones appear on the following pages. Each query is reprinted exactly as it was written when I mailed it to the magazine. Each resulted in a published article. Read them over carefully and see if you can figure out why they elicited go-aheads.

Now let's place these queries under a literary microscope and examine them more closely. You'll notice that all three queries have the following traits in common:

Date. On your letterhead stationery, type the date in the upper right-hand corner. If you don't have a letterhead, you must include the following information on three separate lines above the date: your street address; city, state, and zip code; and your phone number with area code.

Editor's name. In most cases, you can find this information in *Writer's Market* (just make sure it's a current edition. Editors are notorious job-hoppers). If *Writer's Market* lists an editor-in-chief as well as a managing editor, address your query to the latter. He or she probably is more closely involved with the selection of articles. Better yet, if the name of an articles editor is listed, address your query to that person. Do not send your correspondence to publishers. Publishers almost never have a direct involvement with the editorial content of their magazines. That's an editor's job.

October 13, 1976

Mr. Arthur Darack, Editor
CONSUMERS DIGEST
6316 N. Lincoln
Chicago, IL 60659

Dear Mr. Darack:

For many people, flying is a scary experience. But so,
too, is trying to work your way through the maze of complicated fares, discounts, and charters which the CAB has
established for commercial aviation today.

That's why I would like to suggest an article entitled
"Flying at a Discount: How to Bring the Cost of Air Travel
Down to Earth."

For a good many Americans, air travel is still a luxury.
But it doesn't have to be. The airlines have literally
dozens of cheapie fares, although in many cases, they are
reluctant to make them known to the public. True, travel
agents play an important role in steering the consumer
toward reduced rates, but many of these special fares require considerable advance notice in order to take advantage
of the savings.

This article will provide your readers with an easy-
to-understand, no-nonsense approach to air bargains. Point
by point, I'll describe these discounted fares (such as excur-
sion plans, night discounts, adult standy-bys, no-frills
service, and OTC charters), explain how much money they can
save, and provide the restrictions which are attached to
each fare. I'll also zero in on the new ABC charter rates
which go into effect this month, and promise to be one of
the biggest bargains in air fares yet.

My qualifications: for four years I worked as a ticket
agent for American Airlines at O'Hare and have consistently
kept abreast of the recent developments. I have written several aviation related articles including one for PSYCHOLOGY
TODAY and another for CHICAGO. In researching this piece,
I'll use information supplied by the CAB, the airlines, and
reputable travel agents specializing in bargain air fares.

Sincerely,

David Martindale

February 8, 1977

Ms. Phyllis Starr Wilson, Mgn. Editor
GLAMOUR
350 Madison Ave.
New York, NY 10017

Dear Ms. Wilson:

What's the No. 1 complaint of urban residents according to several recent federal studies, including a national survey of renters and homeowners made by the Department of Housing and Urban Development? Well, surprisingly enough, it wasn't high food costs, pollution, or even crime in the streets.

It was noise.

The roar of air conditioners, the incessant bustle of traffic, the annoying blare of the rock music on a neighbor's stereo. As Americans, we are certainly no strangers to this ear-jolting cacophony. In fact, we're assaulted daily. But few people ever realize that continued exposure to noise can prove physically harmful--that the stresses which plague our bodies as a result can be every bit as damaging as a major illness.

I would like to suggest an article entitled "Noise: The Stress You Can Hear."

Within the last few years, the subject of stress has received wide attention in the media, as well it should. Stress-related diseases are the No. 1 killers in America. But very little attention (almost none according to a ten-year check of the Reader's Guide) has been given to the link between noise and stress, even though the correlation has been documented for some time.

This article will examine an important health question long overlooked and little understood by the general public. I'll go to the medical experts in order to tell your readers why noise is so harmful to the body. I'll give concrete, everyday examples of how noise generates stress and adversely affects health, particularly in large urban areas. And perhaps most importantly, I'll give your readers much needed advice on what to do about noise: how to make the environment a good deal less noisy and how to protect the body from the sounds which do intrude.

I'm enclosing a copy of an article which appears in this month's PSYCHOLOGY TODAY which deals with stress-related illnesses of air traffic controllers at O'Hare Airport. I've written other medical-related articles for NEW PHYSICIAN (psychosurgery) and LIFE & HEALTH (longevity). Additional credits include ARGOSY, OUTDOOR LIFE, PEOPLE, CONSUMERS DIGEST, IN CHICAGOLAND, BRANIFF'S FLYING COLORS, ILLINOIS ISSUES, FARM JOURNAL, AIRLINE PILOT, and CHICAGO.

Sincerely

David Martindale

May 3, 1978

Ms. Marlane A. Liddell, Assoc. Editor
SMITHSONIAN MAGAZINE
900 Jefferson Drive
Washington, DC 20560

Dear Ms. Liddell:

Ever since the energy crisis began, there's been a lot of talk about reducing our reliance on oil by conserving energy. New homes and buildings are far more fuel-efficient than those built ten years ago. But now there's a new trend in construction, a trend which would cut fuel costs by using one of the most abundant resources: the earth itself.

I would like to suggest an article for SMITHSONIAN entitled "Going Under."

Although hardly a boom, an increasing number of subsurface schools, office, libraries, and homes have been constructed in the last few years. Sometimes, these structures require excavation; other times, they utilize holes which have already been dug, such as the abandoned salt mines which have been been converted into living units in Utah. The primary reason for "going under": fuel economy. Since the earth is a good insulator, subsurface fuel bills are often cut by as much as 75 percent. The bookstore at the University of Minnesota, for example, is completely underground, and amazingly requires no heating whatsoever as long as the temperature is above -20°. Skylights, machinery, and people supply all the heat necessary. And the same insulation which the earth provides during winters effectively cools the bookstore in summers.

To be sure, there are problems in going under. Some people experience a feeling of being trapped, which is why there is considerable emphasis on adequate lighting. Also, some areas--swamps and other wet lands, for example--are unsuitable for underground dwellings. But with fuel bills soaring all the time, it's clear that man will increasingly burrow his way into the earth to save energy.

In this article, I'll tell your readers about the underground phenomenon. I'll cite specific examples of such structures, talk to the people who design them and live and work there, explain why these subsurface units are so fuel-efficient, and discuss the problems which they pose. And I'll conclude by analyzing the future of subsurface dwellings in an energy-scarce world.

As way of background, I've written several science articles for leading national magazines. My credits include SCIENCE DIGEST, PSYCHOLOGY TODAY, NEW TIMES, PEOPLE, ARGOSY, OUTDOOR LIFE, GLAMOUR, COSMOPOLITAN, PENTHOUSE, CHICAGO, and FARM JOURNAL. I'm enclosing a copy of an article which appears in this month's GLAMOUR dealing with noise and stress.

Look forward to hearing from you.

Sincerely,

David Martindale

If the listing in *Writer's Market* doesn't include any names, check the masthead of recent back issues or call the publication. If you still can't find an editor's name, you have no other choice but to address your query to "Articles Editor."

Name of magazine and business address. Get this information from *Writer's Market.*

Salutation. Begin your query, "Dear (name of editor)." If you cannot get an editor's name, then start your letter, "Dear Sir/Madam."

The lead. Try to begin your queries with some kind of provocative, eyebrow-raising statement. Make it as snappy and as interesting as possible (but don't *ever* sacrifice fact for flash!). The more tantalizing you make your lead, the greater the likelihood an editor will read your entire query. Generally, this lead should be only one paragraph in length, although occasionally, as in the *Glamour* query, it can run longer.

The title. Following my leads, I always include a one-sentence paragraph that begins, "I would like to suggest an article entitled. . . ." The next step is to think of a title. Take your time. Although editors almost always change the title of your manuscripts before they publish your stories, a catchy query title can accomplish the same purpose as a catchy lead: grabbing an editor's attention.

The crux of your idea. Devote one or two paragraphs to a summary of what your idea is all about. Provide the necessary background information and put the idea into perspective. If you can relate it to contemporary news events, all the better. Also, try to point out why your idea differs from other articles that have been written on the same subject.

The plan of attack. Use the next paragraph to tell the editor exactly what type of information you'll supply in your article. Tell how you plan to go about your research and mention some of the people you plan to interview. Although you should definitely show that you have a feel for the magazine's readership, avoid being presumptuous. For example, don't tell an editor, "This is exactly the kind of article your readers have been waiting to read." Also, it's a good idea to phrase your plan of attack positively. Instead of saying "I want to show that . . ." say "I *will* show that . . ."

Your qualifications for writing the article. Of course, this part of the query is considerably easier to write if you've already been published. If that's the case, you can do as I did and list your credits. You should also include one or two tear sheets of previously published articles with your query, as samples of your writing.

However, if you have yet to tally your first sale, then try touting your qualifications instead. If you're proposing a story on ski injuries, for example, mention that you've been an avid skier for several years. Don't lie and claim to be an Olympic gold medal winner. There's a good chance such "misinformation," as it's known in Washington, might come back to haunt you if you wind up receiving a go-ahead. Just summarize your level of experience or expertise in a sentence or two, and then end the query.

What do you tell an editor if you lack both writing credits and subject expertise? Nothing. Just end your query after you've outlined your plan of attack.

Never tell an editor you're just starting out as a freelancer and have no published articles to your credit. Editors are not fools. By your failure to list your writing credits, they will probably assume that you're unpublished. So don't state the obvious. Editors are already prejudiced enough against novice freelancers. And by all means, avoid appeals for sympathy. Refrain from telling an editor, "None of my queries has worked so far, so I'm really hoping you'll give me this assignment." Such soppy melodrama is for soap operas, not query letters. Be a professional. Write the best query you can, sign it, and toss it in the mail.

Closing. Type "Sincerely," or "Regards," and then your name. Be sure to sign your query before mailing it.

BEFORE YOU MAIL YOUR QUERY . . .

Here's a checklist you should follow for all your queries *before* you mail them:

- Keep your query as brief as possible. Try to limit your letter to a single page (a page-and-a-half at the very most).
- Make sure your finished query is as neat and error-free as possible. Single-space all your queries, and leave an extra line between paragraphs. Also, be sure to leave at least a 1 1/4-inch margin at the bottom of the page.

- Always be sure to keep a copy of your queries for your own files (more on this subject in the next chapter). The cheapest and easiest method of making copies is to use carbon manifolds.
- Type the editor's name, the name of the magazine, and its business address on a business-size envelope, exactly the way this information appears in your query. Be certain that the editor's name is spelled correctly.
- Always enclose a self-addressed stamped envelope (SASE) with your queries. To prepare an SASE, type your name and address in the center of a business-size envelope (use your rubber stamp if you have one). Put a stamp on the envelope and fold it horizontally into thirds. Then tuck it into your other envelope, along with your query.

WRITE, DON'T CALL

As you browse through *Writer's Market* you'll notice that some magazines accept telephone queries. Here's a tip: resist the temptation to phone. *Unless you've already written for a magazine and you know the editor, avoid telephone queries.*

Even when approved by magazines (and few really encourage the habit), phone queries simply are not as effective as written ones—not for beginning freelancers, anyway. Because editors are so busy, you stand a good chance of calling at an inopportune time. What's more, by using the phone, you risk completely botching a potential sale. Unless you're an exceptionally good public speaker, there's simply no way you can thoughtfully outline your idea over the phone. Reading from a prepared text won't help either—it sounds stilted and unnatural.

Most editors prefer written queries because they can be examined during less hectic hours of the business day. A written query gives editors an opportunity to sample your writing ability and style, as well. It also permits them to pass your suggestion along to other staff members for their comments. A phone query, on the other hand, lacks all of these advantages.

So for the time being, forget about using Ma Bell to reach out and touch a prospective editor. Use the postal service instead.

7 Waiting for the Go-Ahead

All right, you've written several promising queries, and you've just gotten back from dropping them in the mailbox. Now what? Do you go back to your typewriter and start preparing some more queries? Or do you sit back and wait for editors to reply?

You should probably do both.

Let's assume you've just mailed three queries. For reasons I'll explain later in this chapter, it's highly unlikely—virtually impossible, for that matter—that all three queries will elicit go-aheads. So if you have other article ideas in mind, you should locate likely markets and begin preparing your new queries.

How many queries should you have "out" at any one time? As a rule of thumb, I would suggest at least five, but no more than twelve. You don't want to get *too many* go-aheads at the same time—not now, anyway. Since you're just starting out, you shouldn't try to tackle more than one article at a time. Later, when you become more adept at writing for magazines, you'll be able to juggle several assignments at once.

So if you have only three queries in the mail, start preparing a few more. If you've already sent out several letters, be patient for a few weeks and wait for your ideas to generate some editorial feedback.

Also, you should be aware of two unwritten rules of query letter etiquette.

Never send the same query to more than one magazine at a time. Of course, if a magazine fails to respond to your query, that's another matter. By all means, submit the idea to another publication. But as a writing professional, you have an obligation to give each magazine enough time to evaluate your idea before you send it elsewhere.

Avoid sending the same magazine two or more queries at the same time. For any given magazine, you should send only one query at a time. So if you have a second query you'd like to send to Magazine X, don't mail it until the editor replies to your first.

KEEPING TRACK OF YOUR QUERIES

Besides writing queries, you'll also have to keep track of them. At any given moment, you should know exactly how many queries are sitting on editors' desks and when you mailed them.

So here's an easy-to-use tracking system which will let you know at a glance the status of all your queries.

Begin by taking three manila file folders. Label one "Queries Outstanding," and place in it copies of all your queries that are currently being considered by various magazines. Arrange them by date, with the earliest ones at the front of the folder, and the most recent ones at the back.

Label another folder "Queries Sent." As soon as you receive word that your idea has been rejected, remove the query from the "Outstanding" file and place it in the back of this second folder. (You might want to first retype the query and send it along to another magazine, but we'll discuss this in more detail later.)

Label your third folder "Queries Hold." Use this file to store rejected queries for which you're currently unable to locate a market.

Your next step is to type and then photocopy a Query Routing Log, a sample of which is shown on the next page. Use this routing log every time you send a previously rejected query to another magazine. This way, you won't make the embarrassing mistake of sending the same query twice to the same magazine.

MANUSCRIPT/QUERY ROUTING LOG

TITLE:_____

Magazine:_____Sent:_____Rt'd:_____

Magazine:_____Sent:_____Rt'd:_____

Magazine:_____Sent:_____Rt'd:_____

Magazine:_____Sent:_____Rt'd:_____

Magazine:_____Sent:_____Rt'd:_____

Magazine:_____Sent:_____Rt'd:_____

Magazine:_____Sent:_____Rt'd:_____

Magazine:_____Sent:_____Rt'd:_____

Magazine:_____Sent:_____Rt'd:_____

Magazine:_____Sent:_____Rt'd:_____

Magazine:_____Sent:_____Rt'd:_____

Magazine:_____Sent:_____Rt'd:_____

Magazine:_____Sent:_____Rt'd:_____

Magazine:_____Sent:_____Rt'd:_____

Magazine:_____Sent:_____Rt'd:_____

Magazine:_____Sent:_____Rt'd:_____

Just clip the routing log to the back of your new query, and then file them both in the "Outstanding" folder.

As you'll quickly discover, some editors will reply much more quickly to your queries than will others. Some magazines respond in just a few days but others may take months. A few don't even bother to respond at all—an unprofessional policy which quite rightly irks the hell out of freelancers. As long as you've enclosed an SASE, the *least* a magazine can do is have the courtesy to say yes or no to your idea.

So what's a reasonable length of time to wait for a response to your query? Six to eight weeks, as a general rule, and longer if so indicated in the *Writer's Market* listing. After this time, you can either send a brief letter to the delinquent magazine, inquiring about the status of your query, or you can retype your query and submit it to another publication. The decision is up to you.

THE REASONS BEHIND THE REJECTIONS

Let's assume Charles and Edna each buy three Irish Sweepstakes tickets. Charles tucks his tickets in a drawer and forgets about them. He's realistic. He knows the odds are against him.

Edna, on the other hand, is certain she'll be a winner. In fact, for weeks, all she talks about are her plans for spending her sweepstakes fortune.

Assuming that neither Charles nor Edna wins the Irish Sweepstakes, which person is more likely to be disappointed by the loss?

As a freelance writer, you're bound to be disappointed if you set your expectations as high as Edna. Granted, the odds of getting a go-ahead from a query aren't as dismal as the odds of winning the Irish Sweepstakes. Still, the odds aren't exactly favorable, either.

For a variety of reasons, the vast majority of your queries will be rejected.

During the first two years of my career, less than 10 percent of my queries earned go-aheads. Even after I was well established as a professional freelancer, this figure never topped 25 percent.

There are a number of reasons why queries fail to elicit go-aheads.

Many magazines are overstocked with articles. In order to be on the safe side, editors often tend to buy more articles than they need. When this surplus gets too large, even good ideas can be rejected outright.

A magazine might have recently published a similar article. This is why it's so important either to.flip through back issues of the magazine or to consult the *Reader's Guide.*

An editor might have already assigned the topic to another writer. This happens quite frequently, and there's no way for you to know what articles a magazine has assigned before your query arrives.

Either the subject or the writing is not suitable for the magazine. These are, by far, the two most common reasons that queries are rejected. Although some editors don't bother to explain their decisions, others do take the time to point out *why* the idea or the writing is unsuitable. When that happens, consider yourself lucky.

ANALYZE YOUR REJECTIONS

Many freelancers destroy their rejection slips; I save mine. I now have four file folders stuffed with hundreds of rejections. It's perfectly understandable if your inclination is simply to throw your rejection slips in the wastebasket as soon as they arrive. But before you toss them away, *be sure to read each rejection slip carefully to see if you can determine why your idea was turned down.*

Unfortunately, such careful reading doesn't do much good if you receive a form letter rejection. For example, *Parade's* form letter rejection reads:

> Thank you for querying *Parade* concerning your proposed article but we have determined it is not for us.
> Wishing you all good luck in placing it elsewhere.

"It is not for us." That tells you quite clearly that your query is being rejected, but it says nothing about why.

Like *Parade*, the *Washingtonian* also uses a form letter rejection, but one which at least offers a brief explanation of why they passed up your idea. The letter reads:

Thank you for giving us the chance to read your query/ manuscript. It is being returned because:

_____ The subject is not right for us.

_____ The writing is not right for us.

_____ We have recently commissioned another writer to do a similar article.

_____ We have recently published a similar article.

_____ It does not work for us, but we're not sure why.

_____ It is a possible subject for us, and the writing is acceptable, but we cannot use it at this time. You may want to try us again on it in six months.

_____ We hope you will try us again soon on something else.

_____ We probably never will be happy with one another; please do not try us again for at least a year.

_____ This is an affront to civilization.

At *Washingtonian*, the editor places an "X" in the box beside the appropriate explanation. This method of responding to queries is hardly personalized. But at least you're given some hint as to the reason for your rejection.

Fortunately, many editors take the time to send personal letters of rejection, rather than relying on form letters. For example, a *Penthouse* editor once responded to one of my queries by writing:

This is an excellent proposal, but I'm afraid that we already have more "serious" nonfiction articles in the bank than we have space for, and so I have to reluctantly pass it up.

Clearly, at the time I queried, *Penthouse* was overstocked but at least the editor let me know he liked my idea.

Even when your query is off-target, some editors take the time to tell you why. What's more, they'll often encourage you to send other story ideas. For example, shortly after querying *Passages* with a suggestion for an article on Washington's "old girl network," I received the following letter from the magazine's editor:

> Thank you for writing to *Passages* magazine. I appreciated your story suggestion but found that it is a bit too Washington-oriented for our audience. Most of our audience is business oriented, and while they may be interested in who holds the power, male or female, in Washington, they're more apt to be turned off by the specific problems of women in the bureaucracy—the business bureaucracy might be a different case, but that's another story.
>
> Even though yours is not the right story for us, I hope you will submit more story ideas in the future. We're always looking for stories from Washington, and I quite frequently find myself searching for good writers located in that area. I'm looking forward to hearing from you.

If only every rejection were that detailed and that encouraging. Most are much less than that. Consider the following rejection from the editor of a medical magazine, a publication I queried with a suggestion on the medical uses of hypnosis:

> From the "folksy" tone of your letter, you don't seem to realize that our readers are *all* physicians. Try your next query a bit more on the level of our readers, and I will consider it.

Obviously, this editor had little use for my idea and even less for my "folksy" style. For this reason, I did not query him with additional ideas. Interestingly, had I received a standard form letter rejection from this editor, I might have kept up my approaches to the magazine, never realizing that I was wasting my time since they clearly did not care for my writing style.

So pay attention to your rejections, especially the personalized ones. Learn from them. And if an editor nixes your idea but encourages you to send more queries, by all means do just that. No editor in his right mind would offer such encouragement if he felt your writing was, for instance, "an affront to civilization."

REJECTION TODAY, ANOTHER QUERY TOMORROW

Immediately after you analyze your rejection, you should reach for your *Writer's Market* to see if you can send the same idea to another publication. In many cases, you'll be able to retype the original query, merely changing the name of the editor and the magazine. But you may have to reword it slightly to reflect the different editorial focus of the second magazine.

For example, consider again the ski injury idea. If your first query was sent to a city magazine, it should have been written with a general audience in mind—readers who, if they do ski, probably do so only a few times each year. If you're now planning to recycle that idea to a skiing magazine, you should rework your query to reflect a more sophisticated audience—readers who are often serious amateurs, or even professional skiers. In short, your query will have to assume that the reader of the skiing magazine knows a great deal more about the subject than the reader of the city magazine. If your query suggests that you'd be talking "down" to the ski mag's readers, you can be sure the editor will reject your idea.

By all means, be persistent. If your query is rejected a second time or even a third, keep trying to locate other markets, and send out your query again. In December 1975, I came up with an idea for an article called "Blue Chip Restaurants: Ten Tips for High-Class Dining." At the time, I was working as a waiter, and I was well aware that many people are intimidated by high-class restaurants. They don't know how to get the best table, how to order, or what to tip. So I decided to query a few magazines with a "how-to" suggestion written by a restaurant "insider."

Disappointingly, my query was rejected by editor after editor. Most were encouraging in their comments; the consensus seemed to be that it was a good idea. Yet for one reason or another, each editor felt it just wasn't right for his particular publication. Finally, after sending that query to twelve magazines, I received the go-ahead from a small Chicago-based "giveaway" magazine. I wrote the story and netted $100. After fourteen months of querying and thirteen tries, my persistence finally paid off.

SOMETIMES, EVEN THE BEST OF IDEAS . . .

Unfortunately, there are times when even never-say-die tenacity fails to convert a query into a go-ahead. All too often, many ideas simply never pan out. For example, in 1979, I wrote a query on energy audits—free or relatively inexpensive home surveys aimed at trimming fuel bills. I knew the idea was timely. Energy conservation was a hot topic that year, and the subject of audits hadn't received much attention in the press. So when I typed the query, I was reasonably confident that sooner or later, some magazine would ask me to go ahead with the article.

I was wrong. Despite the fact that I queried half a dozen magazines, the energy audit idea was rebuffed politely by each. Eventually, I exhausted the potential markets for the story and consigned it to my "Queries Hold" file, where it remains today. Should home heating bills begin to soar precipitously again in the next few years, I'll resurrect the idea and try again. But for now, it's just one of many queries that failed to evoke that elusive prize called a go-ahead.

ON SPEC, ON ASSIGNMENT

"Hello, Dave? This is Marty Engels at *Trendy Topic* magazine. Listen, your query sounds very interesting and we'd like to have you go ahead with it."

Whether you receive the news over the telephone or in the mail, your reaction will be the same: elation. So go ahead and celebrate. Call your friends and pour some champagne. You have reason to rejoice.

71

But after you're done celebrating, remember this: Receiving a go-ahead doesn't mean that a magazine will automatically purchase your completed manuscript. It only means a magazine is interested in reading your finished article—*nothing more.*

Fortunately, most editors don't give out go-aheads frivolously. They realize that a freelancer will have to do a great deal of work to prepare that manuscript. For this reason, editors generally ask to see a completed article only when they're reasonably certain the piece will be suitable for the magazine.

Basically, there are two types of go-aheads. One is called "writing on speculation," or "on spec" for short. What this means is that although the editor would like to examine the completed manuscript, he is no way committing himself to purchasing your article. Hence, the speculative nature of the go-ahead. If the editor likes the piece and feels it's suitable, then he will, of course, buy it and send you a check. But if for whatever reasons, he decides *not* to purchase your article, he doesn't have to pay you a penny for your efforts. If this happens, your only recourse will be to take your completed manuscript and try to market it elsewhere. Not surprisingly, "on spec" go-aheads are usually given to novice freelancers who have few, if any, writing credits.

The other type of go-ahead is a full-fledged assignment. Such an assignment should always be spelled out in a written contract. Some magazines, such as *Reader's Digest*, for example, provide form contracts, which the writer is asked to sign. Others, such as *Glamour*, send a short letter outlining the terms of the assignment (see the examples on the following pages). If an editor gives you an assignment over the telephone, ask him to send you a contract for your files. You can save yourself a lot of hassle later if both you and your editor have a clear understanding of the assignment *before* the article is written.

When the contract arrives in the mail, read it over carefully. It should always indicate the subject of the article, the date when the manuscript is due, and the fee that the magazine will pay if the article is accepted. Because the article is on assignment, the magazine will also guarantee you a certain amount of money in case the article is *not* accepted. This sum is called a "kill fee," and usually amounts to 10 to 33 percent of the agreed-upon purchase price of the article.

72

THE READER'S DIGEST

ASSOCIATION, INC.

AGREEMENT
FOR READER'S DIGEST EDITORIAL OFFICE

November 27, 1978

Mr. David Martindale
1321 South Carolina Ave., SE
Washington, D.C. 20003

Dear Mr. Martindale:

This contract when accepted by you, constitutes an agreement between The Reader's Digest Association, Inc., and you, with respect to the literary work entitled   Where Mass Transit Works

(hereinafter "the Work"), as follows:

1. You hereby grant to The Reader's Digest Association, Inc., its subsidiaries and licensees (hereinafter "RDA") exclusive worldwide periodical rights in and to the Work including the right to condense and adapt the Work for publication in all languages throughout the world and to license all the rights granted hereunder to third parties. You also grant the right to reprint the Work and adaptations and condensations thereof in RDA anthologies and compilations, in RDA's educational publications, promotional materials and in reprints.

All other rights in and to the Work remain your property, except that you agree that RDA has the right of first publication in any printed form in any country in the world.

2. RDA shall be the copyright owner of the exclusive rights purchased herein.

3. RDA shall have the right to use the name, biography and likeness of the author in connection with the publication and promotion of the Work.

4. You warrant that you own the rights conveyed herein or are the copyright owner's duly authorized Agent, that you have the full power to grant such rights, that the Work does not infringe any copyright or rights of any third party, or contain any matter that is libelous or otherwise in contravention of law.

5. In full and complete consideration for the rights herein granted, RDA will pay you the sum of

$ ▊▊▊ upon acceptance; $ ▊▊▊ guarantee or kill fee and reasonable expenses

If the foregoing meets with your approval, please acknowledge your agreement by signing and returning one copy of this contract at your earliest convenience.

Very truly yours,
THE READER'S DIGEST ASSOCIATION, INC.

Rosalie Anne Joy
Editorial Business Manager
Rosalie Anne Joy

AGREED AND APPROVED:

By *[signature]*
Authorized Signature

Date 12/8/79

PLEASE RETURN THIS COPY

GLAMOUR

May 3, 1978

Mr. David Martindale
526 West Roscoe
Chicago, Illinois 60657

Dear David:

This letter, when countersigned by you and returned to us,
will serve as an agreement between you and Glamour Magazine.
You will deliver to us an article tentatively titled "Minor
Tranquilizers," following the lines we discussed. The article
will be approximately ████ words long and will be delivered
on or about May 8, 1978. If the article is satisfactory, we
will pay $████ on acceptance for all North American magazine
rights. If it is unacceptable, and cannot be satisfactorily
revised, we will pay a kill fee of $███.

Please keep the copy of this letter for your files.

Sincerely,

Rona Cherry

David Martindale

May 18 1978
Date

Condé Nast Building, 350 Madison Avenue, New York, N.Y. 10017 / (212) 692-5500

Many "how-to" books on freelancing suggest you negotiate resale rights before you sign a contract. My advice is, don't bother. Unless you're Norman Mailer or Gail Sheehy, you're usually going to have to live with whatever rights are outlined in your contract. (For a more thorough discussion of this subject, see the introductory section of *Writer's Market*.)

Although beginning freelancers must generally write "on spec," while the professionals write on assignment, there's really only one major difference between these two types of go-aheads: if the article written by the pro is rejected, at least he's guaranteed a kill fee. Certainly that's an important difference. If an accepted article would have netted $1,500, it's far better to earn $500 if it's turned down than nothing at all. For both writers, however, there is always the risk of having the completed manuscript rejected, even though the query elicited a go-ahead.

So no matter what type of go-ahead you receive, *always make sure you understand exactly what kind of article your editor wants* before *you begin your writing.*

KNOW BEFORE YOU GO

Regardless of whether or not you sign a contract, there are four areas of concern that you and your editor must clarify before you begin working on your article:

The payment. Usually, this is fairly straightforward. You should know what amount the magazine will pay if it accepts your article, and what amount—if any—it will pay as a kill fee. You should also know when you will receive payment: on acceptance, on publication, or sometime in between. If you're to submit illustrations along with your article, find out whether the magazine will pay you extra for your photos (this policy varies from one publication to another). If the magazine will reimburse you for some of your research expenses—i.e., long distance phone calls, photocopying charges, travel—find out which costs actually will be covered, as well as the maximum amount of expense money the magazine will pay.

The length of the article. This may or may not be spelled out in your contract. If it isn't, be sure to ask the editor, ahead of time, what length would be suitable. Some editors want you to adhere as closely as possible to the suggested word length. Others are more flexible. For example, when writing my first article for *Reader's Digest*, I toiled for days trying to cram a great deal of information into just 1,500 words, the usual length of a *Digest* article. Finally, I called my editor and admitted I was having a problem squeezing so much information into such a tight word restriction. Her response was, "Don't worry about length. Send us a long article, and we'll do the editing ourselves." Once I became aware of this policy, my article was considerably less difficult to write.

The deadline date. If you're writing on assignment, you'll almost always be given a deadline. In many cases, you and your editor will negotiate this due date. If so, leave yourself plenty of time. After all, you want to do everything possible to submit your article on time. If, for whatever reason, you feel you won't be able to meet your deadline, by all means call your editor and tell him. Better to ask for an extension than to submit an inferior article just to meet a deadline. Usually you'll find that editors will grant you at least a few extra days.

When you're writing "on spec," editors seldom specify a due date for your article. In this case, just write a letter to the magazine explaining that you will be going ahead with the article, and indicate approximately when you will have the manuscript completed. Don't say, "I'll have it for you by December 15." Say instead, "You should have the article by mid-December, by the end of the month at the latest." As long as the editor doesn't bind you to a rigid deadline, you should give yourself as much flexibility as possible.

Focus. Your query is going to be the primary road map for the focus of your article. If an editor gives you a go-ahead and doesn't provide any special instructions, then write your piece exactly as you said you would in your query. Often, however, editors will give you either oral or written instructions regarding a slightly different slant to the article than the one you suggested in your query. Pay close attention to such advice. Failure to do so is probably the most common single reason why completed manuscripts are not accepted. If an editor tells you to downplay Point A and highlight Point B, you'd best do just that, or your completed article might net you a rejection instead of a check.

8 Research: Sleuthing for the Facts

Now that you've snared your first assignment, your next step is to begin your research. It's a step you cannot avoid. Even if you do boast a certain expertise in your topic, you're still going to have to supplement your own knowledge with quotes and additional facts. If you decide to write your article off the top of your head, your manuscript will almost certainly be rejected. Just as college instructors are adept at detecting "padded" essays, editors possess an uncanny knack for spotting poorly researched articles. Short-cut your research, and you'll wind up short-cutting your career.

Basically, your research will consist of searching for two types of information, printed and oral. This chapter examines written information and where to find it. In the next chapter, I'll discuss interviews: how to get additional information by quizzing the experts.

My decision to focus on printed information before discussing interviews is not arbitrary. As a general rule, you should always collect as much background information on your subject as possible *before* you conduct your interviews. The more thoroughly you do your homework, the richer the dividends will be once you begin your interviewing.

BEFORE YOU SLEUTH . . .

The first thing you must do, even before you begin your research, is get organized. By this time, you should already have earmarked a file folder for this article. In this folder should be a copy of your query—your road map—which you'll want to consult from time to time to make sure your article stays on course. Your file should also contain whatever printed materials you've collected on the subject so far, i.e., newspaper clippings, other articles, reports, etc.

Your next step is to head for the typewriter and prepare a Source Sheet (a sample source sheet is shown on the following page). When you finish typing it, make several photocopies for your files. On this sheet, jot down the name, title, employer, address, and phone number of every individual who assists you in gathering your information. This way, if you need to contact ·these people later for additional information, you'll have a handy reference sheet that will tell you exactly how to reach them. In fact, years from now, while preparing another story, you might want to go back and contact a source who assisted you on your first article. To locate that person, all you'll need to do is head for your article file and pull out your Source Sheet—no long, frustrating searches for phone numbers scribbled on a dozen different sheets of paper.

Finally, before you begin your research, take a moment to collect your thoughts. Using a question format, jot down the major categories of information you're seeking. For example, after I received the go-ahead from *Glamour* for the noise and stress article, I listed five broad questions around which I focused my research effort:

- What is noise and how is it measured?
- At what levels does noise become a nuisance? A health hazard?
- To what degree do high noise levels affect health?
- What is known about the link between noise and stress?
- What can the average young woman do to make her environment a bit less noisy?

SOURCE SHEET--ARTICLE_____#_____

NAME_____   NAME_____
TITLE_____   TITLE_____
ADDRESS_____   ADDRESS_____
_____   _____
CITY_____   CITY_____
PHONE_____   PHONE_____

NAME_____   NAME_____
TITLE_____   TITLE_____
ADDRESS_____   ADDRESS_____
_____   _____
CITY_____   CITY_____
PHONE_____   PHONE_____

NAME_____   NAME_____
TITLE_____   TITLE_____
ADDRESS_____   ADDRESS_____
_____   _____
CITY_____   CITY_____
PHONE_____   PHONE_____

NAME_____   NAME_____
TITLE_____   TITLE_____
ADDRESS_____   ADDRESS_____
_____   _____
CITY_____   CITY_____
PHONE_____   PHONE_____

NAME_____   NAME_____
TITLE_____   TITLE_____
ADDRESS_____   ADDRESS_____
_____   _____
CITY_____   CITY_____
PHONE_____   PHONE_____

NAME_____   NAME_____
TITLE_____   TITLE_____
ADDRESS_____   ADDRESS_____
_____   _____
CITY_____   CITY_____
PHONE_____   PHONE_____

By compiling such a list, I was able to get a fairly good idea as to what kinds of information I would need to gather during my research.

FIRST STOP: THE LIBRARY

Although I've always been a city boy, I will certainly concede that there are a great many advantages to living in a smaller community. However, the freelance writer who is based in a major metropolitan area usually has an advantage over his small-town counterpart. One reason: in most cases, the larger the city, the better the library.

Presumably, you're already familiar with your local library and the services it provides. If not, introduce yourself to a few of the librarians and ask them to acquaint you with the facility. A good librarian can be an invaluable ally who can often save you hours of time and frustration by showing you precisely where to look for a certain piece of information. For this reason, whenever you need assistance at the library, ask a librarian to help you.

Usually, your first task at the library will be to locate a number of general articles on your topic that can be useful in providing background information. For example, when I received my assignment to do the noise and stress article, I set out to find other articles that had already been written on the general subjects of noise and stress.

When looking for magazine articles on your topic, consult the *Reader's Guide to Periodical Literature*, as well as *Access*, a similar periodical reference, which indexes many publications not listed in the *Reader's Guide*. Ask your librarian how you can examine back issues of the magazines you need. Don't overlook newspaper articles, either. The *New York Times* publishes an annual subject index, as do other major papers. Back issues of newspapers are usually stored on microfilm and can be examined with the help of easy-to-use microfilm machines.

Once you locate articles that may be useful in your research, photocopy them for your files. Most libraries provide coin-operated photocopying machines for use by their patrons. (The same is true, in larger libraries, for microfilmed material.) Just be sure to bring along plenty of change. Depending upon how many articles you want to photocopy, you could end up spending a few dollars, but the cost is worth it. You'll save a great deal of time and hassle in the long run by keeping copies of these articles in your files.

After you check for appropriate magazine and newspaper articles, you should also consider examining any reference books that might be pertinent to your subject. For example, if you're writing an article that deals with the growing number of Americans who no longer vote, you should examine a reference book called *America Votes: A Handbook of Contemporary American Election Statistics*. Once again, if you need assistance locating any reference materials, ask your librarian.

Finally, you also might want to check out the library's card catalog to see what books—if any—exist in your area of research. A word of caution, however. Because the pace of events is so rapid today, many books are already dated by the time they appear on the shelves. So be sure to check the copyright date before you consider using the book as part of your research.

COMPUTERS, RESEARCH, AND YOU

As you probably know, many libraries have installed computer terminals to help patrons locate various research materials. If your local library has such a computer, by all means, learn how to use it. You don't need to be a systems analyst to sit down in front of one of these terminals and retrieve a wealth of valuable data. A few simple entries will make the screen come alive with information.

Since 1978, when I moved to Washington, D.C., I've been using SCORPIO, the computer system at the Library of Congress, to aid me in my research. SCORPIO is comprised of four separate retrieval banks, which contain the records of 3.5 million books, 350,000 selected periodicals, all recent legislation enacted or con sidered by Congress, and the member organizations of the National Referral Center. This latter information bank holds the names, addresses, phone numbers, and areas of expertise of over 13,000 organizations and clearinghouses, which offer information to the general public. Fortunately, the services of the National Referral Center are available no matter where you live. Just call the Library of Congress at 202-287-5670. A staff member will assist you in tracking down organizations that might be helpful in researching your particular article.

Many big-city libraries provide access to The Information Bank, a computer-based service of the New York Times Company. The Information Bank contains not only article abstracts from the *New York Times* since 1969, but also the abstracts of over eighty general news, business, foreign-affairs, and science publications from as early as 1971. There is a charge for this service, so check with your librarian.

If you're writing a medical or health article, consider using MEDLARS, the computerized literature retrieval services of the National Library of Medicine. MEDLARS contains over four million references to journal articles and books in the health sciences field that go back to 1965. Over six hundred universities, medical schools, and hospitals around the country subscribe to the service. Should you wish to take advantage of MEDLARS, contact your nearby university's medical library to see whether they're a subscriber. If not, they can probably tell you who is.

Finally, should you happen to own a home computer, you might want to explore the possibility of subscribing to one of the growing number of telephone-linked information retrieval services. Firms such as The Source, CompuServe, and DIALOG Information Services provide a variety of useful data banks, to which you can, for a fee, gain access merely by making a few simple entries on your home keyboard.

BUILDING A HOME REFERENCE LIBRARY

Although you probably haven't gotten around to installing a computer terminal next to your typewriter, I strongly recommend you keep the following five reference books somewhere nearby.

A current almanac. Do you need to know the population of San Diego? the salary of the attorney general? the winner of the Pulitzer Prize for fiction in 1976? No matter what the subject of your article, an almanac will probably provide at least some information which will be useful in your research. In fact, this reference book is so helpful that you might want to spend an hour or two just casually flipping through an almanac in order to reacquaint yourself with the variety of information it contains. Updated paperback editions are available in bookstores each fall.

National Directory of Addresses and Telephone Numbers (Bantam Books). Although this large-format, paperback publication bills itself as the "number one essential reference book for executives," it could just as easily be labeled the "number two" essential reference book for freelance writers (top billing will always belong to *Writer's Market*). The *National Directory* contains fifty thousand telephone numbers and addresses of corporations, newspapers, hospitals, government offices, insurance companies, hotels, embassies, colleges, hot lines, associations, unions—the list goes on. A "must" for any serious freelancer.

Washington Information Directory (Congressional Quarterly, Inc.). Whether you live in Bangor, Birmingham, or Boise, the *Washington Information Directory* belongs on your bookshelf. Why? I'll explain later in this chapter, but for now, suffice it to say that this reference book lists more than five thousand information sources in three categories: Congress, agencies of the Executive Branch, and private, nongovernmental associations. The directory not only provides a capsule description of each organization and agency, but it also tells you exactly where to write, where to call, and which person to contact in order to obtain the information you're seeking. Two exhaustive indexes at the back of the book are cross-referenced by the name of the agency/organization as well as by subject. This annual publication is not inexpensive— the 1981–82 edition, for example, costs $27.50. But considering its value to the research-hungry freelancer, that steep price tag is a bargain.

To obtain a copy, order one through your bookstore or contact the Book Sales Department, Congressional Quarterly, Inc., 1414 22 Street N.W., Washington, DC 20037.

New York Times Guide to Reference Materials (Popular Library). A handy aid to locating information, this paperback book can be found—where else?—in the reference section of larger bookstores.

Zip Code Directory (Arrow Publications). Handy, but not crucial. Available in paperback in many bookstores.

Depending on your area of expertise or specialization, you also might want to stock your bookshelf with other handy reference books. For example, if you wind up writing a number of science articles, then you'll probably want the *Dictionary of Science* (Dell Publishing Co.). If your specialty is health articles, you'll need a reference book such as *The Family Medical Encyclopedia* (Pocket Books).

Also, you might consider subscribing to specialized magazines in your field of interest. Since so many of my articles deal with aviation, I subscribe to *Aviation Week & Space Technology*, a highly regarded journal which is not available on the newsstands. After reading each issue, I save the magazine for future reference. And although the subscription price is fairly expensive, the magazine has paid for itself many times over. I'm able to find not only valuable research information in *Aviation Week*, but also a fair number of ideas for articles.

ASK UNCLE SAM

Pity the poor forests. No one's ever quite been able to figure out how many trees must be sacrificed each year just to keep Washington supplied with paper. But you can bet your bloated government that somewhere, in some godforsaken cubbyhole on Pennyslvania Avenue, some bureaucrat is probably preparing a report on the subject at this very moment.

And therein lies an important point. Sooner or later, the United States Government prepares a report on just about everything. What's more, these reports are available free of charge, merely for the asking.

Here are just three examples of how Uncle Sam has assisted me with my article research:

• In 1979, *Glamour* assigned me to write an article on such do-it-yourself medical devices as blood pressure kits, pregnancy test kits, and electronic thermometers. The agency of the federal government charged with monitoring these devices is the Food and Drug Administration (FDA). Using a telephone contact obtained from the *Washington Information Directory*, I phoned the FDA's press office and asked for help—and I got it. As a result of that one phone call, I was able to obtain an FDA publication entitled "Everything You Always Wanted to Know About the Medical Devices Amendment"; a "talk paper" on pregnancy test kits; three thick reports on electronic thermometers; and the names and phone numbers of FDA scientists who were available for interviews.

• While researching an article for a men's magazine on chemical warfare weapons, I learned that Senator Gary Hart (D.-Colo.) was trying to force the army to remove aging nerve gas weapons, which were being stored at Denver's Rocky Mountain Arsenal. I phoned the senator's press aide in Washington and asked if he could provide any printed data on the controversy. I received dozens of newspaper clippings from Colorado papers which thoroughly outlined the Rocky Mountain Arsenal controversy, as well as some press releases on the subject issued by Senator Hart.

• After receiving an assignment from *Outdoor Life* to write an article about lightning protection, I decided to contact the National Oceanic and Atmospheric Administration (NOAA), the federal agency which researches the weather of the United States and studies meteorological phenomena. A quick call to the NOAA's Office of Public Affairs yielded a number of highly detailed reports on lightning. In fact, the NOAA even supplied me with several 8 × 10-inch black-and-white photographs, which I was able to send to my editor along with my manuscript.

Whatever the topic of your article, be sure to check the subject list in the *Washington Information Directory* to see if the federal government can assist you in your research. If you don't own a copy of the *Directory*, check the reference section of your library. You can also consult the government's *own* directory, The *United States Government Manual* (the *Directory* is preferable, however, because it contains a subject index; the *Manual* does not).

Uncle Sam also prints two free monthly publications that can tip you off to other sources of information:

Selected U.S. Government Publications. Each sixteen-page booklet describes dozens of publications issued by the U.S. Government Printing Office (GPO). Most publications cost less than $10, and an order blank is provided at the back of each booklet. Typical of the publications available are *Smoking, Tobacco & Health: A Fact Book; Occupational Outlook for College Graduates; Solar Power from Satellites;* and *Toxic Chemicals and Public Protection.*

To add your name to the GPO's mailing list, write to the Superintendent of Documents, U.S. Government Printing Office, Washington, DC 20402.

Monthly List of GAO Reports. The General Accounting Office (GAO) is an independent, nonpolitical agency of the government, charged with a watchdog role over the federal bureaucracy. In keeping with this role, the GAO conducts investigations of many government agencies and services. The results of these investigations are summarized in the GAO's reports.

Often labeled with lengthy titles, these reports cover such topics as "World Hunger and Malnutrition Continue"; "Improvements Being Made in Flood Fighting Capabilities in the Jackson, Mississippi, Area"; "Hospitals in the Same Area Often Pay Widely Different Prices for Comparable Supply Items"; and "Disparities Still Exist in Who Gets Special Education."

To obtain the *Monthly List of GAO Reports*, write your request on your letterhead stationery to the U.S. General Accounting Office, Document Handling and Information Services Facility, P.O. Box 6015, Gaithersburg, MD 20877. To find out whether or not the GAO has issued a report on a specific subject, call the GAO Documents Division at 202-275-6241.

ASSOCIATING WITH ASSOCIATIONS

The next time you're at your local library, locate the out-of-town telephone directories and flip through the Yellow Pages for the District of Columbia. Under the heading "Associations," you'll find over fifteen hundred organizations listed, which easily makes Washington, D.C., the association capital of the country. In fact, there's even an association of associations! It's name, not surprisingly, is the American Society of Association Executives (ASAE), and its membership roster includes over six thousand associations from all over the country. Such associations can often provide you with valuable research data.

Are you writing an article that deals with the population explosion in underdeveloped nations? Associations such as the International Planned Parenthood Federation and the Population Crisis Committee might be able to supply you with useful information.

Do you need to know how many blacks own their own construction firms? You might want to speak with someone at the National Association of Minority Contractors.

Trying to track down information on alcohol abuse among Navajo Indians? Chances are, the Association of American Indian Affairs can assist you in your research.

When researching your article, always check to see if there is an association that deals with your subject area. You can locate these associations in one of three ways. First, you can call the ASAE at 202-626-2723. Ask for Information Central and tell the ASAE staff member the subject you are researching. He'll be glad to give you the names of appropriate associations.

You can also examine the *Encyclopedia of Associations* in the reference section of your library. The first volume of the *Encyclopedia* is indexed by subject and key word. The address, phone number, and description of purpose is provided for each association.

Finally, you can consult your own home reference library. Many associations are listed in the *Washington Information Directory*, the *National Directory of Addresses and Telephone Numbers*, and the almanac.

CAMPUS CONTACTS

Each year, America's colleges and universities engage in thousands of research projects. One might relate to the subject of your article. For example, in the late 1970s, the University of Minnesota's Department of Civil and Mineral Engineering was involved in monitoring the energy efficiency of Williamson Hall, the school's underground bookstore/records building. Knowing this, I contacted the university while researching my *Smithsonian* article on earth sheltered architecture and was able to obtain reports, photos, interviews, and leads on other experts in the field.

Unfortunately, there is no central clearinghouse which can alert you to which school is researching what. For this reason, keep an eye open when you're reading through the clippings, articles, and reports you gather. If you read about ongoing or past research conducted at a particular college or university, consult the *National Directory* to find the phone number of the school. When you call, ask to speak with someone in the Office of Public Affairs, and request any printed data on the project that the school is willing to make available.

You should also be aware that many of the larger universities and colleges often prepare "expert lists" which are distributed free of charge to journalists upon request. These lists provide the names and telephone numbers of faculty members available for interviews; usually, they are indexed according to the area of expertise of each professor.

To obtain such expert lists, select several large, well-known universities or colleges and write a brief request on your letterhead stationery. After the lists arrive in the mail, store them in a special file marked "University Experts."

CORPORATE STRATEGIES

Frequently your quest for information will lead you to the public relations departments of corporations and businesses. Like the federal government, these firms can be extremely helpful in meeting your research needs. For example, while researching a story for *Frequent Flyer* called "Jets of the 80s," I phoned Boeing to obtain information about the Seattle-based manufacturer's two new aircraft, the 767 and 757. From that one call, I received nearly a dozen thick booklets, describing both planes in great detail.

Obviously, you're going to have to weigh the merits of the information which you receive from any corporation. After all, the whole purpose of a public relations department is to ensure that the company appears in the best possible light. For this reason, you'll have to carefully separate the facts from the fluff.

Still, you shouldn't hesitate to ask a corporate public relations department to assist you with your research. In the public's mind, PR people are often viewed as shifty-eyed snake charmers with all the scruples of used-car salesmen. From my own experience, however, I've found most PR people extremely helpful and surprisingly honest. As long as you avoid approaching them with a hostile attitude, you stand a good chance of getting exactly the kind of information for which you're looking.

THE LETTER VERSUS THE TELEPHONE

Now that you have a reasonably good idea of what government agency, association, university, or corporation may have the data you want, how should you go about getting it? Should you write or should you phone?

In most cases, you're probably better off phoning, especially if you're under a tight deadline. Letters are easy to ignore. Phone calls can trigger prompt responses. It's true that long-distance phone rates are somewhat expensive—particularly during prime-time business hours, when you'll be making most of your calls—but the cost of the calls is tax-deductible each year. And, once you begin writing stories on assignment, your editor will almost always agree to foot the bill for your calls as part of your expenses.

Presumably, you already know where to look for the appropriate phone numbers. However, if you're still unable to locate a particular number, just dial 411 for local directory assistance, or (area code)-555-1212 for long-distance information. Oftentimes, you'll know in advance the name of the person with whom you'll be speaking. If not, then consider this piece of advice.

When calling a public relations department or office of public affairs, begin your conversation by saying, "I'd like to speak to someone who handles inquiries from the news media." Occasionally, you'll be asked to explain the nature of your inquiry so your call can be routed to the appropriate person—so be prepared to outline your topic in a few brief words. When that person comes on the line, he or she will answer the phone by saying something like, "Hi, this is Mark Jacobs (or Vicky Larson). May I help you?" (Make sure you jot down the person's name for your source sheet.)

Begin by introducing yourself. "Yes, Mark, my name is Dave Martindale. I'm a freelance writer in Washington. I'm writing a story for *Trendy Topics* magazine on the subject of widgets, and I was wondering . . ." Then proceed to outline your request, whether it be for printed information or for an interview with one of the organization's personnel.

If the person you need to speak with isn't in the office, simply leave your name and number, so he can return your call. Occasionally, you'll be asked whether it's all right if the individual calls you collect. You can either agree to this request or you can say you'll call back later. Be persistent, though. If your phone calls aren't returned within twenty-four hours, try again.

If you decide you'd rather type a letter than place a phone call, always use your letterhead stationery. Use a standard business-letter format, and begin by introducing yourself and outlining your research needs as specifically as possible. Whereas over the phone, your source can quiz you if he's unsure of exactly what you need, he has no such option if you query via letter. So be precise.

While preparing an article for *ASTA Travel News* on first-class air travel, I sent eleven letters to major airlines, requesting specific information I needed for my research. A copy of one of these letters appears on the following page, and it should give you a

April 21, 1977

Manager, Public Relations
AIR FRANCE
1350 Avenue of the Americas
New York, NY 10019

Dear Sir/Madam:

I wonder if you could help me?

I'm currently researching an article on first-class air travel for ASTA TRAVEL NEWS, the trade industry publication which is sent to travel agents. My editor has asked me to contact several leading carriers to obtain comments to the following questions:

1. How has the demand for first-class changed during the last ten years? Could you provide statistics to show this trend?

2. To what does AF attribute these changes?

3. Has AF altered the seating capacity of its first-class sections to reflect this change in demand?

4. Do certain routes show a greater demand for first-class than others? If so, which ones?

5. Briefly, could you provide a profile of your typical first-class passenger?

6. What future does AF foresee for first-class?

If you'd like, feel free to jot down any responses on the back of this letter. Also, should you care to comment on any other aspect of first-class air travel--the Concorde, for example--please do so.

Since my deadline is May 20, I would prefer a response at your earliest convenience. Thank you very much.

Sincerely,

David Martindale

good idea how to phrase your correspondence. As a courtesy, you should also consider enclosing an SASE with your letter, especially if you're writing to a private individual, as opposed to an organization.

Finally, no matter whether you're writing or phoning someone for help with your research, remember, *always ask your information contacts if they can recommend any other person or group that might be able to provide you with further assistance in your research.*

Even if the person you contact cannot provide the information you're seeking, that individual may know someone who can, so always ask.

DEALING WITH THE DELUGE

Depending upon the topic you're researching, you may find yourself struggling to squeeze still another inch-thick document into one more overstuffed file. If your file begins to weigh so much it threatens to give you a hernia . . . well, don't despair. Consider it an occupational hazard of a research-thorough free-lancer. It's always better to have more information than you'll need for writing your story.

Of course, sooner or later, you're going to have to wade through all that information and digest it. To assist you in this task, the next time you're at a drugstore or stationery store, buy a felt-tip, "read through" highlighter, preferably in yellow. Then read each of your documents highlighting those facts, phrases, sentences, and paragraphs containing information applicable to your article. Don't be frightened by thick tomes. If Uncle Sam sent you a three-hundred-page technical report, you probably won't have to read the whole report to find the information you need. Just make sure you read the summary thoroughly. If certain sections of the report seem more germane to your needs than others, check the table of contents and read only the appropriate chapters.

Once you've digested all of these materials, head for the type-writer and begin compiling a list of all your highlighted facts. Whenever possible, try to divide this list into subheadings. For example, while organizing my information for a *Frequent Flyer* article on aviation fuel, I divided my research into eleven areas: what *is* jet fuel?; current fuel usage; future cost and availability predictions; recent cost increases; fuel usage of older aircraft; fuel usage of new aircraft; what the airlines are doing to save fuel; what the FAA is doing; how fuel is purchased and distributed; alternative jet fuels; and effect of fuel costs on airline profits.

For the sake of clarity, designate a separate sheet of paper for each of your subheadings. Once you get the hang of it, you'll find this "divide and conquer" technique will not only help you better organize your research, but will also make it considerably easier for you to write your article.

OBTAINING PHOTOGRAPHS AND ILLUSTRATIONS

Although most magazines will not require you to submit photographs along with your article, a few magazines will refuse even to consider your article unless you can provide pictures with your text. In some cases, photos aren't mandatory, but they can enhance the saleability of your article and even earn you extra cash.

One way to obtain photographs for your article is to take the pictures yourself. Then again, you may not know very much about photography. For that matter, you may not even own a camera. (More on cameras in Chapter 14.) Even if you do, you'll be hard pressed to photograph California's Diablo Canyon nuclear power plant if you're based in Fort Lee, New Jersey.

So what do you do if your editor insists that photographs accompany your article?

Basically, the rule for obtaining photographs is the same as the rule for obtaining information: ask. Outline your photo needs to representatives of appropriate associations, businesses, universities, and government agencies.

Consider these examples:

• In 1980, I needed to locate some illustrations for a *Frequent Flyer* article about the Concorde. So I phoned British Airways and Air France, the Concorde's only two operators, and within days, I had several black-and-white as well as color pictures of the needle-nosed SST.

• To illustrate my "Flattop Fires" story in *Firehouse* magazine, I wrote a letter of inquiry to the U.S. Navy at the Pentagon. Within two weeks, I received several highly dramatic black-and-white photographs of the aircraft carriers mentioned in my article.

• Following a go-ahead from *Airline Pilot* to write an article on Chicago's Midway Airport, I contacted the Chicago Department of Aviation and was able to obtain a superb aerial photograph of Midway, showing the airport's layout and runway patterns quite clearly.

All of these photos were obtained free of charge in exchange for a photo credit in the magazine. (Example: Photo courtesy of British Airways.) Occasionally, the contributing organization will request that the photographs be returned after they're used. If that's the case, then write a note to your editor when you submit your manuscript, telling him where to return the photos once the magazine has finished with them.

Although you may not know an f-stop from a shutter speed, that shouldn't stop you from getting precisely the photos you need to illustrate your article—as long as you're resourceful in your search.

9 Interviews That Work

By this time, you should begin to qualify as a miniexpert in whatever subject you're researching. No doubt your file is bulging with printed information. Presumably, you've distilled the most important facts onto several sheets of typewriter paper. As a result, you now have a far more extensive knowledge of your subject than you did when you began your research.

Although you may know a great deal more about your topic than the average layman, you still have to track down a few people who know even more. In short, you have to locate the experts and ask them if they'll consent to an interview. Depending upon the subject of your article, you may also have to interview nonexperts who boast firsthand knowledge of a particular subject or event. (If you're writing about toxic chemical dumps, for example, you might consider speaking with residents of the Love Canal area in Niagara Falls.)

To be sure, interviews can be a hassle. They take time to arrange, time to conduct, and time to process afterward. But if you want to pursue a career as a fulltime freelancer, there's no way you can avoid doing interviews. You can't simply "lift" quotes from other publications. As a professional journalist, you're obligated to credit a publication any time you "borrow" a quote. You can hardly write your own article prefacing each quote by a statement such as, "Recently, Miles Vernon told the *Miami Herald* . . ." And quite obviously, you can't fabricate quotes either, attributing them to "knowledgeable insiders."

Although you've collected considerable printed information for your article, your job is only half complete. Now it's time to get started on your interviews.

THE PURPOSE OF THE INTERVIEW

There are two primary reasons why interviews are so important. *Interviews provide you with additional information for your article.* Interviews pick up where your printed research leaves off. They permit you to quiz the pros and clarify any questions or contradictions which may have popped up during your research. In this way, interviews add authenticity, as well as perspective, to your article.

Interviews yield quotes which can greatly enhance the readability of your article. For example, in my 1977 article for *New Times* about the high-stress world of air traffic controllers, I could have written the following sentence:

> Controlling air traffic is often such a nerve-racking task, that once they finish their shifts, many controllers head straight for the nearest bar, rather than going home to their wives and families.

Although that sentence would have been factually accurate, I opted not to use it. Instead, I decided to quote a 40-year-old ex-controller who had worked for several years in the busy control tower at Los Angeles International Airport:

> "When we left work, it wasn't *are* we going to drink," says Bradford, "but *where*. We used to get off at 7 in the morning and drink very lightly until 1, just sauced up on beer. Then we would start to do some heavy drinking. When you get done talking to 500 airplanes, you just can't go home and go to sleep. You have to have a beer or a scotch-and-water, or else you do as some guys do, and reach under the seat of your car and open a bottle."

The difference between Bradford's account and my earlier description is essentially one of style, not substance. Because he was able to speak from firsthand experience, Bradford not only personalized the subject of controllers and drinking, but he also narrated his account in a way that had a far greater impact upon the reader.

Good quotes make a forceful impression upon the reader. They liven up an article, sustain reader interest, and provide a much-needed change of pace from the uninterrupted monotony of straight prose. Although the number of quotes you'll use in any given article will vary, more is not necessarily better. You don't want to quote people so indiscriminately that your article becomes little more than a series of quotations strung together by transitionary prose. What matters is not the *number* of quotes, but the *quality*. And that quality is dependent upon three variables: your own ability to ask the right questions, the articulateness of your subject, and your ability to know a good quote when you hear it.

THE WHO AND HOW OF ARRANGING INTERVIEWS

From the information provided in the previous chapter, you should have a fairly good idea of where to begin tracking down experts who might consent to an interview. University professors, government bureaucrats, corporate bigwigs, scientists, association executives—these are just a few of the individuals who are appropriate candidates for interviews.

Such contacts can also help you to locate any nonexperts you may wish to interview for your article. For example, while writing a story on teenage suicide for *Glamour*, I wanted to interview several young men and women who had attempted to take their own lives. So I enlisted the aid of staff members at various suicide prevention hotlines. As a result, I was able to interview several would-be suicide victims, some of whom I quoted in my article (to protect the identities of these individuals, I used pseudonyms).

Keep in mind that if you're writing an article that is in any way controversial, you have a journalistic obligation to present both sides of the debate. Depending upon the publication for which you're writing, you don't necessarily have to remain rigidly objective. Some magazines prefer advocacy articles in which the author stands on a soapbox and crusades for a particular cause. (All three of my *Reader's Digest* stories, for example, were "crusader" articles.) Yet fairness demands that you interview at least one person—preferably more—who can plead the "opposing" side in the controversy.

The easiest way to arrange an interview is to use the telephone. When you call your subject, identify yourself as a freelance writer, and explain the nature of your assignment. Then simply ask the person if he would consent to being interviewed. Although the vast majority of people usually agree, some will, on occasion, decline the offer for a variety of reasons. If that's the case, you probably won't have much luck trying to persuade them to change their minds. Everyone has a right to say no to an interview with the press, and, as a journalist, you must respect such a decision.

If your subject agrees to being questioned, you have two options for conducting the interview: you can speak with the person either by telephone or in person. Phone interviews are most commonly used when the writer and the subject reside in different cities. Even if your subject lives on the next block, you still may opt to conduct a telephone interview, especially if you have only a few questions to ask. (More about phone interviews later in the chapter.)

You should be aware that in most cases, meeting a subject in person can yield a much more productive interview. A face-to-face interview is more personal. You're not just a voice on the phone—you're a flesh-and-blood human being, someone who's taken the time to pay a personal visit. For this reason, your subject is likely to be far more cooperative. After all, it's a lot easier to be curt and rude to a journalist over the phone than it is if the writer is sitting in the same room.

Meeting a person face-to-face gives you the opportunity not only to *hear* what the person has to say, but also to observe the way the person speaks. Actors know only too well that communication consists of more than just words flowing back and forth between two people. It is also comprised of subtle, telltale body language—gestures, glances, and movements that tend to confirm or contradict the words being uttered. You cannot observe such nonverbal communication over the phone.

Finally, a face-to-face interview offers you a chance to see your subject in his own environment. This has several advantages. For example, while researching the article on tornadoes for *Science Digest* I decided to interview Dr. Theodore Fujita, professor of meteorology at the University of Chicago. Because I was living in Chicago at the time, I asked Dr. Fujita if I could visit him on campus and speak with him at his office. He consented.

During the course of our conversation, Dr. Fujita continually referred to charts, diagrams, and photos, all of which made it easier for me to understand the thrust of his research. After the interview was over, I was offered a tour of the professor's laboratory. I was even given a demonstration of a "tornado machine" which he had invented to simulate the destructive patterns of twisters. Before I left, the professor lent me an extraordinary 35mm color slide of a Midwest tornado, a photo which *Science Digest* used to illustrate the back cover of the magazine.

In the case of Dr. Fujita, I arranged the interview by calling him directly. Another option would have been to contact the public affairs office at the University of Chicago and ask a staff member to act as a go-between to arrange the interview for me.

As a general rule, the greater the status of the person you wish to interview, the greater the likelihood you'll need to locate a go-between to set up an interview appointment for you. This go-between will usually be someone who is involved in some form of public relations.

For example, if you want to interview the senior vice-president of a textile firm, you're probably better off calling someone in the firm's public relations department and having that person arrange the interview, rather than calling the individual directly. One of the primary responsibilities of any public relations specialist is to act as a link between the press and executives within a corporation (or school, association, government agency, and so forth). Public relations people are not only skilled at arranging such interviews, but they're also likely to be far more cooperative than the boss's secretary, whose primary task is to prevent the boss from being bothered by pesty people like writers.

INTERVIEW DO'S AND DON'TS

No matter whether you conduct your interviews over the phone or in person, here are some tips to keep in mind.

• Always go into an interview prepared. Do your homework; know as much about your topic as possible. Don't try to "wing" an interview by asking questions off the top of your head. Write out your questions in as logical an order as possible *before* your interview.

• If you're conducting a face-to-face interview, be sure to dress appropriately. If you're interviewing a judge in his chambers, you should wear a suit or a skirt. If you're interviewing a rock star, skip the stuffy attire and don a T-shirt and your favorite pair of jeans. In short, you want to try to dress so that you blend in, not stand out.

• Always be honest about the thrust of your article. If you're interviewing a Pentagon official about the danger that Titan missiles pose to the U.S. civilian population, don't mislead the individual by saying you're writing an overview on nuclear preparedness. You stand a much better chance of obtaining the most candid replies if you level with your interviewee.

• Except when you're actually asking questions, spend most of the interview listening, not talking. Be sure to listen closely. Keep asking yourself, Is this person answering my questions forthrightly or is he evading them? If he *is* answering you candidly, then make sure you understand his replies. Many experts eschew ordinary English in favor of technical jargon. If your interviewee tries to do this, politely ask him to "translate" his answers into everyday vocabulary. And whether you're interviewing someone whose answers are evasive or simply elusive, be prepared to ask as many follow-up questions as necessary until you get a straightforward and easy-to-understand reply.

• Be sure you understand the meaning of three journalistic phrases: "on the record," "off the record," and "not for attribution." Because most of the people you interview will be veterans of previous encounters with the press, they'll understand that their conversations are "on the record." If, however, you're dealing with someone who is unaccustomed to speaking to journalists, you should tell the person that you may quote him or her in your article. Occasionally, a more sophisticated interviewee will impart certain information "off the record." Usually, this means you can use such information to supplement your background knowledge, but that it shouldn't appear in print. However, to prevent any misunderstanding, you should take care to clarify this point with your subject. When someone insists that his comments are "not for attribution," you are free to use the quotes in your article *provided* you do not attach the person's name to the quotations. Instead of saying, "According to John Wilson, public affairs director of the Packard Tool & Die Company, . . ." you would write, "According to a spokesman for Packard Tool & Die Company. . . ."

• Whenever you're given a time limit for an interview, do your best to honor that limit. However, watch for signals—both verbal and visual—that your subject might be willing to talk longer. If the person seems receptive, request a brief extension (assuming, of course, you have further questions you'd like to ask). And whether you're under a time constraint or not, you should always try to let the person know when the interview is winding up. Once I finish about three-fourths of my questions, I usually tell my subject, "I have a few more questions I'd like to ask." Usually, I'm done with the interview within five to ten minutes.

• Never pay for an interview. The news is not for sale. You can buy your subject a few drinks, even foot the tab for dinner, but if your subject asks for money, refuse.

• Always be sure to obtain the title of the person you're interviewing. The title may be formal—deputy director of the Eaton Research Laboratory—or informal—an unemployed carpenter. It may be long—acting deputy project manager for chemical demilitarization and installation restoration—or short—homemaker. Titles are important because they identify the people you quote in your articles. For example, mention that someone named Bob Williams called the mayor of Boise a tax cheat, and your reader is liable to wonder why that should be of any particular interest. But if you identify Mr. Williams as, say, the executive director of the Idaho Revenue and Taxation Department, chances are your reader won't dismiss the accusation as lightly.

101

• When you're finished with your interviews, ask your subjects for their home or business address. This way, you can have a copy of the magazine sent to them once your article appears in print. To follow through on your promise, send your editor a list of all the people you interviewed and ask that each person be sent a complimentary issue of the magazine when your article is published. Most publications will comply gladly.

• Occasionally, a subject will ask to review his comments *before* you submit your article. If you wish to comply with such a request, you don't have to send the person your entire article. Instead, you can send a copy of only that portion of your article in which the individual's quotes appear. If there's any dispute over what should or shouldn't be included in the article, talk the matter over with your editor.

BE A CONFIDANT, NOT A JUDGE

If you watch any television at all, you're probably quite familiar with confrontational interviews, the type that has often been associated with CBS journalist Mike Wallace of *60 Minutes* and fictional newspaper reporter Joe Rossi of *Lou Grant*. The principle of this kind of interview is that when interviewing a "hostile" subject, the journalist should be equally hostile, if not downright abrasive. The questions are often so loaded that the viewer doesn't even have to bother listening to the replies. (For example, "You mean to tell me your company is *not* extorting Social Security money from little old ladies?") Why should the TV viewer care *what* the subject answers? From the strategic, holier-than-thou, guilty-until-proven-innocent attitude of the journalist, the viewer already assumes that the interviewee is guilty as hell.

Because confrontational interview techniques are such good theater, they work well on television. After all, who *doesn't* enjoy seeing shifty-eyed corporate villains squirming under tough questioning? If, however, the purpose of an interview is to elicit as much information as possible—even from the "hostile" subject— then the go-for-the-jugular technique surely rates as the worst method of interviewing, because, in most cases, subjects who are confronted with hostile questioning don't *open* up, they *shut* up.

From my own experience, I've found that the best method of interviewing people is to ask tough questions, but in as noncommittal and as nonjudgmental a fashion as possible.

Even if you're convinced that the person you're interviewing is an unscrupulous liar, don't tip your hand. If you appear as though you're suspending judgment, your subject will be far more inclined to confide in you. But, if your body language or the tone of your questioning suggests contempt for the man and his comments, you're unlikely to get the information you're seeking.

For example, while researching the article on behavior modification programs in prisons for a major men's magazine, I heard a number of wild allegations about a certain psychiatrist at a prison in Washington State. This psychiatrist—I'll call him Dr. X—was director of the prison's Mental Health Unit, a pseudo-psychiatric ward charged with providing "therapy" to "problem" inmates. One former "patient" of the MHU said of the experience, "It was the only time in my life that I felt I was going to die." This prisoner went on to recount some of the horror stories which allegedly occurred in the MHU:

> "I saw people beat up and have buckets of water thrown on them, including dirty mop water. I saw pitchers of hot coffee thrown on people—people stripped and hand-cuffed behind their backs. I saw a cup of piss thrown on a guy that was in a strip cell. I saw people being led around in diapers with ropes around their necks, being put in a prone position on their toes and elbows, and then kicked in the ribs when they would fall down."

Eager to confront Dr. X and ask him about these allegations, I arranged to interview the man when I visited Walla Walla in late 1977. Dr. X resembled a lovable old granddad—a tall, gaunt man in his mid-60s, whose graying hair was trimmed in a sort of crewcut.

Instead of adopting an accusatory line of questioning during the interview, I opted to play the role of devil's advocate. Although I asked some tough questions, I made sure I prefaced each with a statement such as: "According to your critics . . ."; "I've heard charges that you . . ."; and "What would you say to those people who claim that. . . ." Eager to gain a sympathetic ear and tell *his* side of the story, Dr. X took two hours, explaining every allegation. In so doing, he only confirmed that the horror stories I had heard about the MHU were, in fact, true. Among the doctor's most scary quotes:

"I've trained horses, and there isn't any difference between training a horse and training a person."

"A penal institution is a baby-sitting operation. When a prisoner acts infantile, we put him in a playpen by himself. When he thinks he can come out of that cell and act like a man instead of a spoiled brat, we let him out."

"The only way to treat these individuals [prisoners] is to circumvent their rights."

I have no way of knowing for sure, but I'm convinced that if I had used the confrontational method of interviewing, Dr. X never would have confided in me the way he did. But because he *did* confide in me, I was able to include some truly Orwellian quotes in my article.

So when you're interviewing, save your judgments for your writing. That doesn't mean you shouldn't ask tough questions— fire away! But be mindful of your attitude. Outwardly, you should appear as neutral as possible during the interview, even in you're convinced—as I was in Walla Walla— that you're talking to a truly dangerous human being.

THE NOTEPAD VERSUS THE TAPE RECORDER

Unless you have a photographic memory, you'll need to find a way to record the quotes and information provided by your subject during an interview. Two options are available. You can either take notes, or you can record the interview on a cassette tape recorder. In my opinion, the second option is clearly preferable.

Taking notes during an interview is a distracion, one which can severely jeopardize your rapport with your subject. Even if you know shorthand—and most freelancers don't—you'll spend so much time and mental energy jotting down the words being spoken that you won't really have time to *listen* to your subject. If you're interviewing someone in person, note-taking prevents you from maintaining eye contact and watching the person's body language. What's more, note-taking can lead to inaccuracies. If you take notes during an interview, you can never really be sure if you've quoted your subject verbatim. You also risk omitting statements or, worse yet, recording them inaccurately.

Using a tape recorder, on the other hand, is a relatively trouble-free method of recording an entire interview verbatim. Simply press the "Record" button, and you can sit back and concentrate on your questions and your subject's responses. If your interviewee reels off a list of detailed statistics, you don't have to interrupt and ask him to slow down or repeat himself. The tape recorder will pick up every word. Better still, the machine will record every nuance in your subject's voice—vocal variations which can significantly shade meaning. In this way, you're recording more that what a person says—you're also recording the *way* in which it's said.

All right, those are the advantages of using a tape recorder. Now for some of the drawbacks.

● Tape recorders cost money—far more money than a pen and notepad. For tips on what kind of cassette tape recorder to buy, see Chapter 14.

● Tape recorders can malfunction. While researching an article for *Cosmopolitan*, I spent 45 minutes interviewing a woman who headed TWA's passenger service operation at JFK Airport. As I do during any interview, I periodically glanced at my tape recorder to see if the wheels of the cassette were still spinning slowly around. The tape was moving, all right, but as I learned later, the machine had recorded only the first ten minutes of the interview. The culprit was my weak batteries. Since this particular interview formed an essential part of my article, I had to call the woman later, and ask to redo the bulk of the interview over the phone. Although she consented graciously, it was still embarrassing for me, especially since it came from a supposedly professional journalist.

Cassette tapes can snap, and recorders can break down. But most bungled tape interviews can be traced to a single cause—

weak batteries. For this reason, *always check the batteries before using your tape recorder. If you're not sure the batteries will last throughout the entire interview, buy new ones.*

• Tape recorders sometimes intimidate people who are being interviewed face-to-face. Although I have found that some subjects are a bit hesitant about speaking in the presence of a tape recorder, most people will consent to my using the machine. Only rarely will anyone refuse. As long as the recorder is placed just out of their view, after the first few minutes, subjects tend to forget it's even there. Treat it nonchalantly and chances are your subject will do the same.

• Tape-recorded conversations must be transcribed later. (More about transcribing later in the chapter.)

Despite these drawbacks, I'm still a confirmed tape-aholic. In fact, I can't, for the life of me, understand how or why anyone would take notes during an interview. Nevertheless, you should probably try *both* methods before you decide which one is right for you.

TAPING AND THE TELEPHONE

Assuming you'll become a tape recorder convert, you'll probably end up taping many of your interviews over the telephone. If so, a word of caution: Ma Bell takes a dim view of telephone tapers. In fact, in most states, it's a violation of phone company tariffs to record any conversation *unless* you use a tone-warning device which beeps every fifteen seconds. Generous mother that she is, it just so happens that Ma Bell will supply you with such a device—for a fee, of course.

Before you call your Bell service rep and order a tone-warning device, consider this: a violation of phone company tariffs isn't an outright illegal act. Rather, it's quasi-illegal, the tariff having the weight, but not the strength, of law. Unless you're an attorney, that probably sounds like so much legal mumbo-jumbo. I agree. Remember, even if you *don't* use a tone device, you're not committing a true crime—as long as the other party is *aware* you're taping the conversation.

You should also be aware that some writers never tell their subjects that their phone interviews are being taped. They believe that taping phone calls has an unsavory reputation and that people may get uptight over the phone if they know they're being taped. For this reason, many journalists rationalize their decision to secretly tape their phone interviews. The argument goes something like this:

If you're a freelance writer (which you are), and if you identify yourself to the person you're interviewing (which you will), what difference does it make if the conversation is being recorded on tape? After all, the person at the other end of the line knows that he's speaking "on the record." He's aware that his statements may be quoted in your article. You could be the most skilled practitioner of shorthand this side of the Rockies, and even though you'd have the ability to jot down your subject's every word, you wouldn't be legally obligated to *tell* him you're a shorthand whiz. What's so different about using a tape recorder to preserve a conversation? People who have a hangup about having their conversations recorded on tape don't realize that a tape recorder is their best assurance they *won't* be misquoted. Why tell them ahead of time if they may balk, especially if using a recorder is to their benefit as well as the writer's?

Of course, if you do decide to tape your phone conversations, you're going to have to resolve these ethical dilemmas for yourself. As for the hardware used in telephone taping, there are two different kinds of devices that will enable you to tape directly from your phone to your cassette recorder. Both are available at electronic supply outlets like Radio Shack.

The first and less expensive device is little more than a long wire with a suction cup at one end and a jack plug at the other. All you do is stick the suction cup on the top (listening) end of your telephone receiver, insert the jack into the microphone socket on your recorder, and you're ready to record your phone calls. Such devices do, however, have two big drawbacks. First, the sound reproduction is poor. And second, such devices allow you very little movement while you're on the phone. Unless you stay right beside your phone, you'll pull the suction cup off the receiver.

A far more effective (and a bit more costly) item is called a telephone recording control. This device hooks directly into the base of your telephone via a clip-style plug. A second wire, leading from the control box, is plugged into your tape recorder. The advantage of this device is that is not only provides much better sound reproduction and a greater freedom of movement, but it also permits you to keep your phone permanently "wired" for tape recording. This way, when someone you've been attempting to interview returns one of your phone calls, you're all set. Just press the "Record" button on your tape recorder, and the entire conversation will be taped.

AFTER THE INTERVIEW IS OVER

If you take notes instead of recording your interviews on tape, you have little work to do once your interviews are completed. Of course, if you have a difficult time reading your notes because you were scribbling so quickly, you should type them out as soon as possible. If, on the other hand, your notes are legible, then all you'll need to do is team them up with your printed research data, and you're ready to begin writing your article.

However, if you tape your interviews, you'll have to transcribe those tapes before you can use the interviews as part of your research. Transcribing tapes can be a time-consuming chore, but the extra work is worth the effort. Although you'll probably have to listen to the whole tape, chances are you won't have to transcribe the entire interview verbatim.

When transcribing your tapes, don't bother typing every single word spoken by your subject. Summarize key facts, and type out only those direct quotes that you think you may use when writing your article.

Granted, it's going to take you a while before you get the hang of transcribing tapes—that's to be expected. But before long, you'll develop an "ear" for transcribing. You'll know precisely which information you should summarize, and which direct quotes might work well in your article.

Don't expect *every* interview to yield exciting quotes. As I've learned from experience, some of the most brilliant people are often the most inarticulate. Although they know what they want to say, they're simply unable to convey their ideas in a way that the average person can understand. Conversely, some of the least educated people can articulate their thoughts better than many Harvard graduates. I once spent three hours listening to an ex-offender whose account of prison life was so vividly detailed and spellbinding that it was hard to select which quotes to use in the article. Nearly every sentence seemed to merit inclusion.

As for your subject's syntax, don't hesitate to alter it a bit if necessary, *provided* you don't change the meaning of what's said. Very few people can speak grammatically perfect English while giving an extemporaneous interview. So if your subject says, "The idea that noise denotes power is a long-term old wives' tale that we've been beset with," feel free to change that sentence to read, "We're beset by an old wives' tale that noise denotes power."

Don't erase the tapes of your interviews until several months after your article appears in print.

There is always the chance—remote as it may seem—that someone you interview will claim he was *inaccurately* quoted. In fact, he may even threaten to file a libel suit against you and the magazine. Since your tape-recorded interview is your best proof of what was actually said, you should keep your tapes for a while rather than erasing them to record other interviews. Although I've never had anyone accuse me of misquoting them—knock on wood!—I still keep my tapes, just in case.

(For a more thorough discussion of interviewing others for publication, see *The Craft of Interviewing* by John Brady, Vintage Books.)

10 From Madness to Manuscript: Preparing Your Article

Like many people, I keep a journal. Every week or so, I take a few moments to jot down comments and observations about many of the events in my life. While rereading my entry for January 5, 1976, I discovered the following paragraph:

As for my *Chicago* magazine article on controllers, I've finally completed all of my research. Thank God! Now the only question remains: What the hell am I going to *do* with all this data? I honestly wonder whether I'm ever going to be able to pack all this information into one magazine article. At times I'm convinced it simply can't be done. But then, I really don't have any choice in the matter. I've *got* to write this article. After all, my editor expects a completed manuscript at the end of the month. I can't just call him up and tell him I can't hack it. I've at least got to *try* to write the article. Still, the whole thing scares me. Maybe it'll get easier once I've had a few articles under my belt, but for now anyway, I'm on the verge of a minipanic. Should be interesting to see what happens.

OVERCOMING THE BLANK-PAPER BLUES

If you're beginning to wonder whether or not you'll ever be able to make any sense out of that mountain of information *you've* acquired, welcome to the club. I know what you're going through. I still have vivid recollections of the "minipanic" that gripped me before I wrote my controllers piece. I've even named this panic. I call it the Blank-Paper Blues, or BPB for short. You might be interested to learn that even though I now have more than a hundred published articles and, now, two books to my credit, I'm *still* plagued by periodic bouts of the BPB. In fact, while glancing over my notes before writing this chapter, I suffered another mild attack:

Oh, my God! I know what I want to say, but how am I ever going to be able to distill all that information into one brief chapter?

Fortunately, I've long since discovered that the simple cure for the Blank-Paper Blues is to start writing.

So here's my advice. Set aside all those self-doubts, worries, and anxieties. Tuck them away in a distant corner of your mind and use your self-discipline to prevent them from escaping. Keep telling yourself you *can* write your article—that, dammit, it's going to be a good article, it's going to be bought by your editor, and it's going to be read with interest by the magazine's readers. Then start writing.

Don't procrastinate. Your article has to be written sooner or later, so you might as well get started today. You may not finish your manuscript for a couple of weeks, maybe even a month or more. That's beside the point. At least you'll have *something* down on paper, and that's a start.

Take heart. Once you've written a few articles, you'll not only develop more confidence in your own abilities, but you'll also become far more adept at overcoming those vexing, somehow inevitable Blank-Paper Blues.

111

BASIC ARTICLE STRUCTURE

You should be aware that most contemporary magazine articles are divided into four distinct sections.

THE LEAD

Ideally, the lead of your article should perform the same function as the lead of your query—to grab your reader's attention. From the first sentence of your article, you want to snare your reader and so involve him in your story that he'll find it well-nigh impossible not to read the whole thing. Your lead doesn't have to be long—usually just a few short paragraphs. But what it lacks in length, it should make up for in impact. Shock your reader, surprise him, make him angry, or amuse him. Stick to the facts, but tantalize him with a hint of what's to come.

Human interest stories often provide excellent subject material for leads. For example, here's the one I wrote for a *Reader's Digest* article, "Where Energy-Saving Is a Way of Life":

> Ed and Marcia Buckman couldn't wait to move out of their large, rambling home in Lodi, Calif. "We were sick of paying over $100 a month in utilities and wasting energy," explains Marcia. "It was crazy!" So when Ed was transferred to Sacramento, the Buckmans decided to look for a truly energy-efficient home.
>
> Fifteen months ago, the couple and their five children moved into a new $75,000 solar home in Davis, a small suburban community 12 miles from Sacramento. "It's like a dream come true," says Marcia. "Our utility bills last winter averaged just $32 a month. And despite summer temperatures that can reach 115 degrees, the house stays comfortable without air conditioning."

The story of Ed and Marcia Buckman proved an ideal lead for two reasons. First of all, it encouraged the reader to identify with the Buckmans—after all, who *isn't* upset by sky-high utility bills?—and second, the Buckman's story showed that unlike other communities, Davis offered an *alternative* to soaring fuel costs, which was precisely the point of my article.

In many respects, the trolley article that appeared in the August 26, 1979, issue of *Parade* was very similar in focus to the Davis piece. In both articles, I examined unconventional solutions to common problems. But with regard to style, the lead of my *Parade* article was much different from the one that appeared in *Reader's Digest:*

> During the last 28 years, the population of Edmonton, Alberta, in Canada, has more than tripled. Not surprisingly, this boom town shares a problem with other large urban areas—monumental traffic tie-ups. Yet Edmonton's method of tackling the problem may be a sign of the future.
>
> Determined to ease congestion in the city's busy northeast corridor, Edmonton officials looked at several options. One was an expensive and unpopular freeway; another, the construction of exclusive bus rights-of-way. Both plans were rejected.
>
> Instead, Edmonton selected the least costly alternative: a $65 million Light Rail Transit (LRT) system, an updated version of yesterday's streetcar lines. Today, sleek two-car trains whisk along the 4.5-mile line in just about 12 minutes, about half the time it takes a bus or car to travel the same route. Says former auto commuter Janice Loomis, "I enjoy the trip because it's fast and efficient. It beats driving."

What's the best lead for *your* article? You'll have to determine that for yourself. Each article is unique. Go back through your research materials and see whether you can locate an intriguing lead. Chances are, there's at least one very good candidate just waiting for top billing in *your* article.

THE THESIS

Following your lead, you should summarize the basic thrust of your article in a single paragraph, two at the most. Tell the reader exactly what you aim to prove in your article. For example, the thesis of my *Reader's Digest* article reads:

It's no accident that such a home [the Buckner's] was built in Davis. Without waiting for a nudge from Washington, this thriving community of 36,000 people enacted the nation's first energy-conservation building code and now ranks as the most energy-conserving city in the country. "In Davis, saving energy isn't a trend," explains Mayor Tom Tomasi. "It's a way of life."

After reading that paragraph, my readers are aware that the rest of the article will be devoted to showing why and how Davis, California, is so dedicated to energy conservation.

The thesis of my *Parade* article reads:

First introduced in the late 1880s, the streetcar flourished during World War I, when more than 44,000 miles of track blanketed the U.S. But as autos became more popular, ridership declined. By the mid-1950s, the streetcar had become an endangered species as most cities abandoned their systems. Today, less than 225 miles of track remain in just eight U.S. cities.

Yet streetcars are now making a comeback in the U.S.— and a timely one, at that. For as gas becomes more scarce and traffic more congested, a growing number of American cities are planning brand-new LRT systems or upgrading existing lines. As a result, LRT seems destined to play an increasingly important role in this country's mass-transit development.

Why did I include a paragraph that summarized the history of streetcars in the U.S.? Because that paragraph gives my thesis a historical perspective. The fact that new streetcar lines are being built in the U.S. would hardly be newsworthy if trolley tracks in America were as widespread as freeways. But they're not. Only by being aware of what an important role streetcars played in earlier years can the reader more fully appreciate the significance of building new trolley systems and upgrading existing ones today.

Such a historical perspective wasn't needed in the *Reader's Digest* article on Davis—readers were already well aware of the energy crisis. They didn't need to be reminded how the 1973–74 Arab oil embargo catapulted the phrase "energy conservation" into the nation's vocabulary. They could appreciate the steps that Davis was taking to conserve energy without being told why such steps were necessary.

Whether or not you need to incorporate a bit of historical perspective into your thesis will depend upon your topic. Give it some consideration before you begin writing. You may find it necessary to provide a few sentences of background information so that your reader can better appreciate your thesis.

THE BODY

This is the longest section of any article, and therefore the most challenging. Now that you've stated your thesis, you're going to have to spend the next several pages proving it. To do that, you'll need to marshal a great many of the facts you've gathered during your research. What's more, those facts will need to be arranged in a logical order and written in highly readable, I-can't-put-it-down prose.

An impossible task? It certainly can seem like one if you begin thinking of the body of your article as a huge, unwieldy, formless mass—some large blob over which you have no control. But if you use the divide-and-conquer strategy that I outlined in Chapter 8, you'll find the body of your article will be easier to write, more logically organized, and considerably more interesting to read.

To see how divide-and-conquer works when you're writing your article, let's go back to the *Reader's Digest* article. The body of the Davis story is divided into eleven separate parts. These various subarticles tell the reader (1) where Davis is located and what type of people live in the community; (2) how in 1966, this increasingly car-clogged city opted to give preferential treatment to bicycles; (3) how this probicycle policy led to an energy conservation building code for the city; (4) why the city's building code is unique; (5) how Davis's contractors reacted to such a radical building code; (6) how the Buckmans' solar home saves energy; (7) what other kinds of new energy-conserving homes are being built in Davis; (8) how older homes there are being made more energy-efficient; (9) how the city's building code has affected Davis' overall energy consumption; (10) what other methods residents use to save energy; and (11) what reaction the Davis experiment has elicited from the Department of Energy.

These eleven subarticles each highlight a different aspect of the Davis story.

The body of the *Parade* article tells the reader (1) why Edmonton's LRT system is so successful; (2) what advantages LRTs boast over other forms of mass transit; (3) how Buffalo is building a brand new LRT line; (4) which other American cities are either building new LRTs or upgrading existing lines; and (5) why LRT lines will probably be expanded in the future.

This time, five subarticles within one body. Never mind that the reader probably never suspects that he's hopping from one subarticle to another. He's not *supposed* to know. If the story is well written, it will flow so effortlessly that the reader will never begin to imagine the organizational skills it took to put that article together.

So remember the divide-and-conquer technique. Use it when you're compiling your research data, and use it when you're writing the body of your article. Your own article may contain just seven subarticles or it might contain as many as seventeen. The number isn't important. The fact that you divide your article into manageable segments *is*.

THE ENDING

I've found that endings are usually more difficult to write than leads. In most cases, I'm pretty sure how I'm going to begin my article even before I complete my research. Endings, for me, at least, are far more elusive. Obviously, endings are extremely important. After all, you can't come to a screeching halt after you've outlined your last fact. You've got to write some sort of finish for your article, some type of conclusion. But what?

Of course, a great deal depends upon the subject of the article. In the Davis story, for example, the ending didn't pose much of a problem. The whole purpose in writing the article was to show how one community could effect significant energy savings without the help of Washington. In closing, I knew I wanted to subtly encourage other communities to emulate Davis.

So after mentioning that the Department of Energy allocates just a fraction of its multibillion-dollar budget for local energy-conservation programs, I concluded:

> Yet localities are the best places to start conserving energy, since household use accounts for 22 percent of all the energy consumed in this country. And local governments exercise important control over such energy-related variables as building codes, permits and land use. More important, localities have the unit of government that is closest to the people. And people—not institutions—determine energy consumption.
>
> The success of the Davis energy program represents a triumph of local initiative over federal inertia. Only when such a grass-roots effort as this spreads will the United States begin to achieve *real* energy conservation.

Keep in mind that it's not always possible—or wise—to hop on a soapbox to conclude every article. Sometimes it's better to let others end your story for you. For example, in the *Parade* article, I concluded with the following paragraph:

> Edmonton is an oil-rich city that has a love affair with the auto. Despite this, LRT ridership has jumped 30 percent in the last year. "The lesson from all this," says Llew Lawrence, Edmonton Transit's director of marketing and development, "is that people *will* use public transit if you make an effort to put it where they want it, when they want it, and make it reasonably comfortable."

What more could I have added to a statement like that? Nothing, as it turned out, so that's where I ended my article. The moral of this *Parade* ending is that sometimes you'll find that the people you interview can do a better job of ending your articles than you can ever do yourself.

117

MANUSCRIPT ON DRAFT

Now that you're familiar with the basic format of a magazine article, you're almost ready to start writing. Before you do, though, sit down and prepare a rough outline of your article. Presumably, you now have a pretty good idea of how you'll begin your article, what you'll include in your thesis, and how the article will end. All that's left is to list the major points that will comprise the body of your article. Just be sure to arrange these points in some sort of logical sequence.

When your outline's complete, grab a piece of the cheapest typing paper you have, feed it into your machine, sit down in front of the keyboard, and force yourself to begin. Keep your research notes handy; you'll be consulting them often.

Don't expect miracles the first time around. Your first draft will probably bear only a faint resemblance to your finished article.

*The secret of good writing is revision. Think of your first draft merely as a starting point—a huge block of stone to be sculpted into a polished piece. With each successive revision, you'll be able to chip away more and more of the rough spots until finally—*voilà—*that hunk of stone is transformed into a flawless masterpiece.*

It's to be expected that first drafts will be riddled with poor writing. So don't despair if your syntax is confusing, your grammar faulty, your spelling abominable, or your organization downright illogical. No masterpiece ever leaps forth from the typewriter on the first draft. The whole *purpose* behind a first draft is to commit your words—rough as they are—to paper. Once these words are written down, *then* you can go back and rework them into a more refined form.

How many revisions will it take before your article is completed? That's difficult to say. At the bare minimum, two. While writing especially difficult articles, I often need to make five or six revisions. Particularly stubborn paragraphs within articles can sometimes require as many as ten revisions. There is no magic number that will work for every story; you'll have to play it by ear and decide for yourself when you're through revising.

Although I prefer to type my rough drafts, you may decide

118

you'd rather write yours out in longhand. No matter which method you choose, just be sure to double-space your rough drafts. Also, don't choke your left and right margins. You'll need plenty of room to make corrections. In fact, from time to time you'll make so many corrections, you'll have to turn over the page and write on the back.

After I finish typing my first draft, I take the manuscript back to my desk and review my research notes to see if I've omitted any pertinent information that should be included in the article. Then I grab a red ballpoint pen and begin making the necessary corrections. As you can see from the sample text on the next page, sentences are deleted, whole paragraphs are shifted around, and words are inserted in the middle of sentences—in short, the draft undergoes a thorough overhaul. When I've finished reworking the entire manuscript, I retype it, return to my desk, and begin the same process all over again. Invariably, the second revision is much easier to accomplish than the first, the third easier than the second, and so on. When a draft finally passes inspection without any revisions, I pronounce the article finished.

No manuscript is ever ready for final typing until it passes one all-important test: *before you type your completed article, always go over your text in detail to double-check your information for accuracy.*

Larger magazines such as *Reader's Digest* employ research specialists whose sole task is to ensure the accuracy of every fact in every article. Submit a manuscript riddled with errors to such a publication and it's a safe bet your article will be rejected outright. Of course, for budgetary reasons, most smaller magazines are unable to thoroughly verify your research. Nevertheless, you still have an obligation as a journalist to ensure that the information you include in your article is accurate. To a large extent, your reputation as a writing professional will depend upon the accuracy of your work.

Granted, inaccurate articles occasionally "sneak past" unsuspecting editors and wind up in print. But you can be fairly certain that some reader somewhere usually spots the inaccuracies and alerts the magazine. If that happens to your article, don't even bother to query the magazine again. Regardless of the merits of your idea, you'll never land another go-ahead there—at least not until the present editors move on to other jobs.

around. ^*Your first draft will probably only bear a faint resemblance to your finished article.*

The secret of good writing is revision. Think of your
first draft as merely a starting point--a huge block of stone
which must be sculpted into a polished manuscript. With each
successive revision, you ~~chip~~ *'ll be able to* chip away more and more of the rough
spots until, finally, voila--that hulk of stone becomes a
masterpiece.

How many revisions will it take you to complete your
story? ~~I'm afraid I can't answer that.~~ *That's difficult to say. At the bare minimum, two.* From my own experience,
while writing a particularly difficult article, I after need to
I ~~know that I'm seldom able~~ to send off a ~~completed~~ manuscript
without ~~at least two revisions.~~ More difficult articles have
Complete required five or six revisions. And in~~dividual sections of~~ *particularly stubborn paragraphs*
Within an articles have ~~often resulted~~ *sometimes required* in as many as ten revisions.
Not surprisingly, First revisions, ~~almost by definition,~~ *drafts* ~~usually~~ *are often riddled with*
in poor writing. ~~(As an example, see the sample first draft~~
That's to be expected. Your ~~is flawed;~~ *imprecise,* ~~on this page.)~~ The syntax, the grammar, the spelling, the *your*
So do I & deeper if *faulty.*
organization--the flaws abound in any first ~~draft. That's~~
To masterpiece ever come spewing out of a typewriter the first time around.
~~to be expected. But at least~~ the first draft forces you to
The whole purpose of the first draft is to commit your ideas to rough as they are
put down something ~~on~~ paper. ~~And once this something is written,~~
then *go back &* *Once those ideas are written down,*
you can change ~~it.~~ *them*
Although I prefer *you may decide you'd rather*
I ~~always~~ type my rough drafts. ~~You may prefer to~~ write
which
yours out in longhand. No matter ~~what~~ method you choose,
just *and leave plenty of room*
~~you be sure to double-space your rough drafts, so that you~~
Also, don't *at the left and right margins. You'll need plenty of*
choke your can leave yourself ~~some~~ room to make corrections. After I *finish*
left & right *typing* *of my rough* *remove the ms from the typewriter, take it*
margins. comp~~leted~~ each drafts, I ~~go~~ back to my desk, and ~~start~~ making
additional *begin*
corrections using a red ballpoint pen. Sentences get deleted,
whole paragraphs are shifted around, words are inserted in

As you can see by the sample on the opposite page(s),

TYPING YOUR MASTERPIECE

Accuracy is only one mark of a professional writer. Another is the way you submit your completed manuscript to your editor. Here are several tips on how to prepare the most professional-looking manuscript possible:

• Use only 16- or 20-pound, 8 1/2 × 11-inch white bond paper—no colored paper, no odd sizes, no erasable bond, and no paper that comes glued to any kind of pad. Use standard-sized, heavy-weight, white bond—*nothing else*.

• Margins should measure 1 1/4 inches on all sides. If your typewriter uses pica type as opposed to elite (pica letters are larger, and standard on most machines), you'll be able to set your tabs so that sixty spaces separate your left margin from your right. You'll also find yourself able to fit twenty-six double-spaced lines on each page. For estimating purposes, assume one full page of text contains approximately two hundred fifty words.

• Paragraphs should be indented five or six spaces from the left margin.

• If your typewriter lacks an "end of the page" feature, make a light pencil mark along the left margin approximately 1 1/2 inches from the bottom of each page. When this mark becomes visible, type your final line on that page. Be sure to go back later and erase each pencil mark.

• The first page of your manuscript should be prepared in the following manner. In the upper left-hand corner, type your name, street address, and city, state, and zip code on three separate single-spaced lines. Approximately one-third from the top, center and type the title of your article in capital letters. Double-space twice and then type the word *by* directly beneath the title. Double-space once, and type your name. Finally, double-space three times and begin typing your article (see the sample first page layout on the following page).

• On each successive sheet of paper, type your last name in capital letters in the upper left-hand corner of the manuscript, approximately one double-space from the top. On the same line, in the upper right-hand corner, type the page number. Then double-space three times and continue typing your text.

David Martindale
526 W. Roscoe
Chicago, IL 60657

NOISE: THE STRESS YOU CAN HEAR

by

David Martindale

Ten years ago, John and Karen Hansen bought a new house.
Today they realize they made a mistake. There's nothing
wrong with the house itself. The two-story brick structure
is well-built, easy to maintain, in a neighborhood they like.

But there is one problem that outweighs all the advantages: noise.

From their kitchen window, the Hansens peer out at the
six-lane expressway that links Chicago's Loop with O'Hare
Airport. Twenty-four hours a day, they're bombarded by the
roar of trucks and the din of automobile traffic. Across
the expressway, high-speed commuter trains rumble toward
the downtown terminal, rattling the Hansen's windows. As
if that isn't enough, their home sits directly beneath the
flight path to one of O'Hare's main runways. For several
hours each day, jets screech overhead at the rate of one

- After you've typed the final sentence of your manuscript, double-space three times and type "---END---."

- *Always make sure you insert a carbon manifold behind each page of your manuscript. You must keep a duplicate copy of your article for your files.*

- No matter how proficient your typing skills, you're bound to make errors while typing your final manuscript. Still, your completed article must be as neat and smudge-free as possible. This is relatively easy to accomplish if you own a self-correcting typewriter. Press a button and any typing error is automatically lifted off the page. If your machine uses a carbon ribbon but doesn't have a self-correcting feature, you should remove errors by using "lift-off tabs," which can be inserted by hand in front of the paper. If you're typing on a machine with a cloth ribbon, use a liquid white-out eraser to camouflage your mistakes. Avoid using any kind of eraser on your manuscript. Also, make sure your cloth ribbon is relatively new. It must print darkly enough for your editor to read your work without straining. Check, too, to see if the holes in the letters *a, e, g, o,* etc., are "inked-in." If so, clean them out before you begin typing.

- Once you finish typing, proofread the entire manuscript. If you spot additional errors—and you will—apply *a little* liquid eraser to your mistake and then type the correction. If you decide to alter a long phrase or an entire sentence, you're better off retyping the whole page.

- When you complete your manuscript, make sure the pages are in the proper order and then clip them together with a paper clip in the upper left-hand corner. Never insert your article into any kind of binder and, by all means, don't staple the pages together. One paper clip is all you ever need.

- *Before you mail any manuscript, ask yourself, Is this as neat and as professional-looking a manuscript as possible? If not, go back to your typewriter and retype the entire article.*

MAILING YOUR MASTERPIECE

Once you finish typing and proofreading your article, you're ready to submit it to your editor. Before you do, however, you should prepare a brief cover letter on your letterhead stationery. Don't use this opportunity to hype your piece—your article will speak for itself. Also, avoid outlining all the problems you encountered while preparing your manuscript. Every article has its share of problems, and it's doubtful that yours were unique. So don't bother crying on your editor's shoulder.

Instead, your cover letter should contain any additional information about the article that your editor might need to know. For example, you might want to mention that if the magazine needs additional photographs, you know where to get them. If you don't have any special information to impart, just write, "Per your recent interest in my query, I'm enclosing my article, 'How to Avoid Ski Injuries.' Look forward to hearing from you."

Your next step is to gather together all the materials you'll be submitting and stack them in the following order:

- Your cover letter.
- Your invoice, if any (more on this subject in Chapter 15).
- Your manuscript.
- Your photos, if any. Be sure to insert a lightweight piece of cardboard behind the photographs to prevent them from being bent.

Once these materials are properly organized, take out a 9 1/2 × 12 1/2-inch or 10 × 13-inch manila envelope and either type or stamp your return address in the upper left-hand corner. Then type your editor's name and the address of the magazine on a plain mailing label. Lick it and place it squarely in the center of the envelope.

If your article was written on assignment, you're all set; you don't have to bother sending an SASE since the magazine will foot the bill for postage if your manuscript has to be returned. Just put your materials in the envelope, seal it, weigh it on your postal scale, and affix the proper postage in the upper right-hand corner.

However, if your go-ahead was "on spec," you'll have to include an SASE with your article. Here's what you do. Take another address label and type or stamp your own name and address on it. Attach it to another manila envelope, and temporarily put it aside. Now put your materials into the envelope you'll be mailing to your editor and weigh it on your postal scale. Then put the appropriate postage on your *SASE*. Fold the SASE in half, and place it in the envelope behind your other materials. Seal the original envelope and weigh it again. Since your SASE adds to the total weight, you'll usually have to add one more stamp than the number you affixed to your SASE.

You may, of course, be tempted to send your manuscript via registered mail, rather than "risking" ordinary first-class. My advice is not to bother. I've found that most of the short-comings of the U.S. mail are greatly exaggerated. In seven years of writing, I've never had a single piece of correspondence lost or misplaced in the mail—not one. So why bother standing in line at the post office and spending extra money just to register your article? It isn't worth the expense *or* the hassle. There is only the remotest chance the Postal Service will lose your manuscript. Even if they do, the world won't come to an end—you still have an extra copy of your article in your files, just in case.

The only time you should consider giving your manuscript preferential postal treatment is when you're concerned about meeting a tight deadline. When that happens, just head for your main post office and send your package via Express Mail. You'll pay a premium for this overnight delivery service, but the extra cost will be worth it if it means the difference between an on-time manuscript and one that is overdue.

Then again, you may not have to rely on the Postal Service at all. If the magazine is based in the same city in which you live, you can always save yourself the postage and drop off the article in person. A word of caution, though. Don't expect your editor to greet you at the door, read your article while you wait, and then issue you a check right on the spot. In fact, it's unlikely you'll even be able to meet your editor face-to-face—not yet, anyway. Instead, you'll probably have to be content to leave your article with a secretary.

Whether you send your article or hand deliver it, you're going to have to wait for your editor to read it. Hardly an easy task, of course, but an unavoidable one, nonetheless.

11 Your Editor and You

Consider the following scenario:

After receiving a go-ahead on your query, you write your article. You then submit it to your editor and wait a few weeks for a response. If the editor likes the piece, the magazine mails you a check. If for some reason the editor *doesn't* like the article, the manuscript is returned to you, and you're free to submit it to other publications.

If only it were always that simple.

This is not to suggest that the above scenario is fictional. It's not. Oftentimes, it's an accurate summary of what really happens, especially when you're writing for lower- and middle-level magazines. With many magazines—particularly the top national publications—the acceptance/rejection process is a bit more complicated. Knowing what to expect ahead of time can help you cope with these complexities. And knowing what to expect from your editor (and what your editor expects from you) can mean the difference between a sale and a rejection.

ACCEPTANCE, CONDITIONAL ACCEPTANCE, AND REWRITES

Regardless of the publication to which you submit your manuscript, your editor will definitely contact you—either by mail

126

or phone—if he decides to accept your article. Don't expect a prompt reply. If the editor contacts you within a week of receiving your manuscript, consider yourself lucky. As a general rule, the average response time is anywhere from two to four weeks. If your editor hasn't reached you within a month, call or write and ask to be advised of the status of your article. In most cases, if you're writing on assignment for an out-of-town magazine, your editor will accept a collect phone call.

Of course, if you're notified that your article has been accepted as is, you can breathe a bit easier. Assuming that you're writing for a "payment on acceptance" publication, your editor will authorize the accounting department to issue you a check for the agreed-upon payment. Occasionally, some magazines will ask you to invoice the publication directly. If you receive such a request, consult Chapter 15 for tips on how to prepare an invoice. If you're writing for a "payment on publication" magazine, you can congratulate yourself on garnering an acceptance, but don't hold your breath waiting for a check to arrive in the mail. It may be months—even a year or more—before your article is actually published.

Sometimes, an editor will inform you that he'll accept your manuscript *if* you're able to provide additional information to supplement the text. For example, I received such a conditional acceptance after I submitted an article on lightning safety to *Outdoor Life*. One paragraph of the acceptance letter read:

> I'd like some additional information. Can you give me your comments about CB and other radio antennae on recreational vehicles and boats? And perhaps a paragraph or so on outriggers, surf rods, and so on. Most of our readers are hunters and fishermen and I'd like to focus more strongly on them and their equipment. You can write this information in the form of an insert and we can add it to your manuscript. Just tell us where in the text you'd like this to be inserted.

The editor went on to say that if he received such information within two weeks, he would authorize payment for the article.

The *Outdoor Life* example is typical of a conditional acceptance. For a variety of reasons, editors often request additional information so that they can better tailor the article to suit the needs of their readership. With a conditional acceptance, you don't have to rewrite your article, but only supplement it with additional facts.

Some editors—especially those who work for the top magazines—will go a step further and return the manuscript, asking for a major rewrite. Should your editor make such a request, this doesn't mean he's decided to accept your article. On the contrary, it means that the way it stands now, your article is unacceptable. Still, you're being given a second chance. Your editor has decided to postpone a decision on whether to accept or reject your piece pending the outcome of your rewrite.

If rewrites sound like a hassle . . . well, they are. But they're one hassle you have to endure if you want your manuscripts accepted. If it's any consolation, remember that the pros probably receive far more rewrite requests than rookies, simply because they're writing for such demanding publications.

Sometimes rewrites are requested because the freelancer failed to write the article in a style suitable for the magazine. Consider my experience with *Glamour*. By early 1978, I had already written two articles for the magazine, both were accepted without rewrites. Later that same year, I wrote three more stories for them. The subjects were longevity, teenage suicide, and self-care medical devices. All three of these articles were returned for rewrites because, although my research was thorough, I failed to personalize the articles for *Glamour*'s readers. Like many publications, *Glamour* prefers that, whenever possible, its writers employ a second-person narrative style. This is a policy I should have known about. After all, it wasn't as if I had never written for the magazine before.

Fortunately, my editor there gave me the opportunity to rewrite all three articles the way they should have been written in the first place. As a result, each was subsequently accepted and later published in the magazine.

At other times, rewrites are requested not because the style of the article is unsuitable, but because the research is incomplete. For example, about a month after I submitted my story on energy conservation in Davis, California, to *Reader's Digest*, my editor returned my manuscript with a three-page letter. In the opening paragraph, she said, "To give the article the best possible chance of success before I submit it to our purchasing editor, would you mind addressing yourself to the following points?" She went on to list, in great detail, eight areas where changes were necessary.

The first time I read the letter, I was angry. My God—I'd just spent *weeks* researching and writing this piece, and what happens? My editor asks for a complete overhaul! Remove this! Add that! I thought I was *done* with this piece, and now here it is sitting right back on my desk again.

Fortunately, good sense prevailed. After a few days, I cooled off—so much so, that I actually began agreeing with my editor that the changes would, in fact, improve the article. Not that the rewrite was a breeze—it wasn't. It took more than a week of work and also required additional research. But since I was determined to earn not only a top magazine credit but also a hefty check, I followed my editor's advice and made all eight changes.

A few weeks after I resubmitted the manuscript, my editor called me to say the article had been accepted. Only later did I realize the extent of my accomplishment. As my editor told me in a subsequent conversation, my original manuscript was so off the mark, she gave me only a 50/50 chance of being able to rewrite it satisfactorily. Thank God she had given me the chance to turn a failure into a success.

Yes, rewrites are a hassle, but they're an inevitable part of any freelancer's career. If you remember this important rule, you will always stand a good chance of converting a would-be rejection into a sale:

Whenever an editor returns a manuscript for a rewrite, make sure you understand exactly what changes need to be made.

If you're lucky, you'll be dealing with an editor like the one who handled my Davis story for *Reader's Digest*—one who spells out in explicit detail what revisions are necessary. Should an editor return your manuscript with a comment such as, "I'm not quite sure what's wrong with this, but I think you should revise it," then quiz him. Tell him to be more specific. After all, *he's* the one who's going to be making the final decision on whether to accept or reject your piece. *He's* the one who should tell you what you can do to improve your chances for a sale.

GOOD EDITING, BAD EDITING

As I mentioned in an earlier chapter, editors are going to edit your manuscripts. That's their job. The purpose of editing is not only to improve the readability of your article, but also to ensure that your research is accurate and thorough. Many editors are, of course, quite skilled at editing. Others are not. Sometimes an editor will make only minor changes in your text. At other times, he'll edit you far more heavily. A lot depends upon your topic and the magazine's readership.

Many magazines have a policy whereby a writer is permitted to review his edited manuscript before it's published. This gives you an opportunity to contest any editorial changes you may not like. By reviewing your edited manuscript prior to publication, you can also ensure that the editing hasn't in any way altered the thrust of your article or the meaning of specific statements.

Unfortunately, not all magazines extend such a courtesy to their writers. *If you would like to review an edited copy of your article before it's published, be sure to ask for such a review. In most cases, the magazine will comply with your request.*

Like many rookie writers, I was unaware of this option when I began writing. In fact, for the first year or so, I never really gave the subject of prepublication review much thought. Then I got burned—not on just one article, but three!

The articles were a story on the metric system for *Braniff's Flying Colors;* a piece on barbiturates for *Family Weekly;* and my iceberg article for *Science Digest.* None of these magazines offered to let me see an edited version of my work. Neither did I ask to review the editing before publication. In retrospect, I wish I had, because all three articles were so poorly edited that I was embarrassed to have my name appear in the by-line. I felt like telling the readers, "Don't blame me! This is my research, all right, but I don't write like this. This is an editor's writing, not mine!"

Of course, I was never able to broadcast such a disclaimer. Nor did I bother to complain to the offending editors. The damage had already been done. My only recourse was to promise myself I would boycott all three publications in the future, a pledge I've managed to keep.

The only advantage to being burned three times in a row is that you learn your lesson well—and I certainly did. A few years later, I wrote an article on acid rain for *Science 80* magazine. After rewriting the piece at my editor's request, I was sent an edited version of the article for review. It was dreadful. The writing was choppy and erratic. It was as though random facts had been strung together without any consideration for flow, let alone logic. Many of the sentences within paragraphs bore no relationship to one another.

Unfortunately, I was too busy with other assignments to haggle with my editor and try to reach a compromise. Nor was I able to withdraw the piece and prevent it from being published, because I already had been paid for the article—the magazine owned it. Left with only one recourse, I wrote my editor and asked that my name be deleted from the by-line and a pseudonym substituted instead. Although I'm still disappointed with *Science 80* for their botched editing job, I'm grateful that the editor complied with my request.

Hopefully, you'll never have to remove *your* name from the by-line because of bad editing. You should be aware you have that option. After all, your reputation as a writer is at stake. When a reader picks up your article, he sees only one name on that by-line—yours. So if you have any complaining to do, do it *before* your article is sent to the printer. And if, after talking the matter over with your editor, you still feel the final version is poor, remove your name from the article. What good is a by-line if the article is an embarrassment instead of a source of pride?

Good writing is a team effort, so try to collaborate as much as possible with your editor during the editing process. And remember, too, that the quantity of editing isn't nearly as important as the quality. Some of my own manuscripts have been so covered with blue pencil marks that I could barely see the typing. Still, I never complain about such heavy editing—as long as I'm convinced the resulting article is an improvement over what was originally submitted.

WHY MANUSCRIPTS ARE REJECTED

Even if you write your article on assignment, that doesn't mean an editor will automatically accept your completed manuscript. For a variety of reasons, both "on spec" and "on assignment" articles are often rejected as unsuitable for publication. Sometimes the editor is squarely to blame for these rejections. Sometimes the writer is the chief culprit. And in many cases, both editor *and* writer are at fault.

There are three basic reasons why manuscripts are rejected.

Editors change their minds. Strange things can happen between the time an editor reads a query and the time he reviews a completed manuscript. A query may sound terrific to an editor in April, but that doesn't necessarily mean he'll hold the same opinion of the completed article in June—even if you *do* write your story exactly as you proposed in your query.

For example, consider this experience I had with one men's magazine. In the fall of 1977, I queried the magazine with a suggestion for an overview article examining the controversy surrounding chemical warfare weapons. After receiving an assignment from the magazine, I wrote the article and submitted it in mid-December.

Several weeks later, the editor returned my manuscript with a letter telling me he had decided to "take a pass" on the article. Despite the fact that I had adhered to my query, he wrote, ". . . I don't think a general overview of the subject will work [for us]." Toward the end of the letter, he candidly admitted that *he*, not I, was to blame for the rejection. His letter went on to say:

> Perhaps it also has something to do with your catching me while [we were] in Chicago [the magazine had since moved to Los Angeles], my looking for *anything* from top

professional writers, and tossing you Nerve Gas without thinking it through as I should have. Whatever, that's behind us. But the point is, if you're not too burned at ...and me, I'd still like to have you write for us.

Although I *was* burned at both the magazine and the editor—instead of earning $1,200 for the article, I had to content myself with a $250 kill fee—I heartily applaud the man for his honesty. Such an admission is rare and refreshing, and showed me that editors, like writers, are, in fact, human.

Even if an editor sounds genuinely excited by a query, that's still no guarantee that the completed manuscript will be purchased. In 1980, I wrote a story for *Parade* about a federal hotline, which had been established to encourage people to report incidents of fraud, waste, and mismanagement in government. I waited several months to learn whether *Parade* would or would not buy the piece; the article was finally returned in the mail. Said the accompanying note, "On a second look, the editors felt [the article] could be boiled down to less than a feature." This rejection came from a magazine so enthused about the idea when it was first proposed that they assigned me the story *the day they received the query*.

Sometimes editors change their minds about a story—even though the idea for the article came from them in the first place. For example, in late 1977, an editor at *Chicago* magazine asked me to write an article about Cook County Jail, the city's infamous, problem-plagued penal institution. I was hesitant about taking the assignment. After all, like most city magazines, *Chicago* is a "coffee-table" publication—a magazine read primarily by the city's more affluent residents. It just didn't seem likely to me that a Michigan Avenue society matron would want to read an article about lower-class, primarily minority convicts being packed into an overcrowded, terror-ridden jail, where physical and sexual assault were daily occurrences. At the same time, reforms at Cook County Jail were clearly long overdue. How could my article plead for such reforms if it were so sanitized, so devoid of the nitty-gritty of daily jail life, that even a penthouse matron would feel comfortable reading the piece?

So before I accepted the assignment, I discussed these questions with my editor. After listening patiently, he assured me that the Cook County Jail article was appropriate for the magazine. "We sometimes run stories which our readers may not want to read, but *should* read." He advised me to write a hard-hitting story and not to worry about what the readers would think. Convinced I had editorial support for the piece, I did exactly that.

It was only *after* I submitted my manuscript that I began to wonder whether my editor had undergone a change of heart about the story. First, he asked for a revision. Even after I did a major rewrite of the article, he was still unhappy with the piece. What it needed, he said, was to be "toned down"—with less emphasis on the vivid vignettes of jail life and more on the upbeat developments at the institution. (What's "upbeat" about a jail in which gangs rule whole cell blocks, guards traffic in drugs, and 18-year-old offenders are routinely subjected to hour-long gang-rapes by literally dozens of convicts?)

Although my editor was willing to let me do a second rewrite, I declined. Convinced that the two of us would probably *never* agree on how the article should be written, I opted to take the kill fee and bow out of the project. Why continue when it was obvious my give-'em-hell approach—one which I thought had editorial support—was only going to result in a rejection?

Unfortunately, there's not much you can do if an editor changes his mind about your article. Nor do you have much recourse when a magazine says it will accept your article, but then re-considers and rejects it after all. (This happened to me twice—once with the *Saturday Evening Post* and once with *Glamour*.) You can complain until you're blue in the face, but in the long run, it's the *editor* who is the final arbiter of what will or won't be accepted.

An editor can change jobs, leaving an article in the hands of another, who may not be as enthused about the piece. In 1978, I received an assignment from *Cosmopolitan* to write a career article profiling several women working in various computer occupations. I'd met with the editor who assigned me the story and knew I had his support. But by the time I had finished writing the article, that person had departed *Cosmo* for a new job. My manuscript was reassigned to another editor on the *Cosmo* staff.

To say that the piece on women in computers failed to excite this second editor is to understate his reaction. Calling the article "drab and repetitive," he returned the manuscript and declined to ask for a rewrite. Although I don't honestly believe the article *was* drab and repetitive, who knows? Maybe it was. Maybe my original editor would have rendered an identical verdict. Yet even if he *had* been disappointed with the piece, I'm fairly confident he would at least have given me the chance to rewrite—and possibly salvage the piece.

Three years after the *Cosmo* incident, I got a similar rejection from *Washingtonian* magazine when it rejected my article on National Airport. It seems that the editor who assigned me the piece had taken a new job, leaving my article sponsorless. Hence, the rejection.

Of course, editorial job-jumping can sometimes be to a freelancer's advantage. If an editor you know moves to a better job at a better publication, you may just find yourself with an "in" at a higher-paying magazine. But as the previous examples illustrate, the career-switch sword cuts both ways. And for a freelancer, the *dis*advantages to editorial job-jumping can often prove costly as well as frustrating.

Writers either don't deliver the article they promised in their queries, or they don't heed the editorial advice given when the piece is assigned. Once again, your query is your road map. Deliver a different article than the one you proposed originally, and you risk having it rejected when the completed piece doesn't live up to initial expectations.

It's also extremely important that you have a clear understanding of what kind of article your editor is looking for. In 1980, one of the editors at *Parade* called me and asked if I would write an overview article on the new computer games and toys that were flooding the market. Intrigued by the idea, I agreed. Yet, shortly after I submitted the piece, the article was rejected. Now that I look back on it, I have no one to blame for the rejection but myself.

To begin with, I never asked to have the thrust of the story spelled out in writing. Instead, I relied solely on one phone conversation to provide a guideline for tackling the piece. That was my first mistake.

Second, I failed to quiz the editor thoroughly to learn exactly what kind of an article he wanted. I'm sure my editor was convinced I understood the assignment. In retrospect, however, I didn't—and that was my fault, not his.

Finally, instead of checking with my editor before I came up with what I thought was a workable angle for the article, I went ahead and wrote the story. Rather than providing an overview on the subject, I spent the bulk of the article profiling six representative computer games and toys. This clearly was not at all the kind of piece my editor had in mind, and I don't blame him for rejecting the article. Had I been him, I would have done the same thing.

The fact that the *Parade* story was written on assignment meant that I was at least able to collect a kill fee for my efforts. The only other consolation for having a piece rejected is that you're free to submit the article to other publications. That's not always easy, however. Since different magazines have different readerships, rejected stories often have to be "reslanted" to reflect these differences. If you do try to pitch a rejected article elsewhere, you may be better off querying first, rather than submitting the entire manuscript. This way, if you get a go-ahead, you never have to mention that the article was written for another magazine and rejected. You can simply reslant it (if necessary) and submit it for consideration.

If one of your articles is rejected, and you're the kind of person who relishes a high-stakes gamble, you still have another alternative. You can always do your *own* rewrite and resubmit the article to the magazine that turned it down in the first place. This is a risky venture—if the editor thought you could salvage the piece, he probably would have suggested a rewrite himself. But if you honestly feel that a dynamic rewrite will lead to a sale, then by all means, go ahead.

GETTING TO KNOW YOUR EDITOR

If you write for a magazine based in the same city in which you reside, try to arrange a personal meeting with your editor.

Face-to-face writer/editor meetings are important because they often lead to long-lasting professional relationships. So if you're writing for a locally based publication, try to meet with your editor in person. Don't expect to be able to sit down and talk for several hours. Occasionally, an editor may call you up and invite you out to lunch. But normally, you'll have to content yourself with a brief, ten or fifteen-minute visit. The important thing is that *you* meet *him*, and *he* meets *you*.

Once you write for a magazine and get to know the editor, you can alter your marketing approach a bit and call him to suggest story ideas. The editor will not necessarily give you an immediate go-ahead, but if he's interested in the idea, he'll probably suggest that it's worth your effort to write a query. If he *doesn't* like the suggestion, he'll let you know right there, over the phone. This way, you won't waste your time querying a magazine that isn't interested in your proposed article.

Perhaps the biggest advantage of getting to know an editor is that, eventually, he may ask *you* to do an assignment. For example, in September 1978, I received the following brief letter from an editor I knew at *Glamour*:

> Dear David:
>   I'd like you to do a feature on fatigue for *Glamour*. Are you interested?
>   We would like to do this as soon as possible. Give me a call and let me know if you have time to do this piece.

I agreed, wrote the story, and earned $1,200 when it was accepted.

A word of advice, however. Don't feel you *have* to take an assignment just because an editor asks you. Shortly after I began my career as a freelancer, the editor of *New Physician* asked me to write a story on the ethics of biomedical experimentation. Without giving the subject much thought, I agreed. After all, I reasoned, an article assignment was an article assignment. What difference did it make *what* the topic was?

Only after I began researching the piece did I realize that I had no real enthusiasm for this particular subject. To be sure, I wrote the story and submitted what I thought was a good article. The piece was accepted and published. But if I had it to do all over again, I probably would pass up the assignment. In my experience, when you tackle a subject that's uninteresting or even downright boring, writing becomes a chore, not a challenge.

AFTER THE SALE

Just because an article is accepted and bought by an editor, don't count on it getting published in the magazine. In most cases, of course, it will be, but many magazines maintain a backlog of articles, any one of which can be used in case a pending article falls through. However, many of these backlogged stories will never get to print.

A year after my behavior modification story had been accepted by *Penthouse*, the article still had not been published. I wrote my editor and inquired about the status of the piece. My letter said, in part, "I'm assuming that because of scheduling problems, the article probably won't be printed." The editor wrote back:

> I'm afraid that your assumption seems to be correct. It's not that the executive editor doesn't like your article (he does, that's why it was purchased), but unfortunately, he seems to like other articles more.

You may never run into this problem during your own career. Still, you should be aware that there's always the possibility that you might receive a check for your article and never see a by-line.

Even if your article *is* eventually published, there's a good chance it won't appear in the issue for which it had originally been scheduled. For a variety of reasons, articles tend to get "pushed back," sometimes one issue, often several. Check with your editor for updates, but be patient with him. It's not easy of course, especially if you're writing for a payment-on-publication magazine. But once your article is accepted, your best bet is to forget about it until it appears in print. Instead, spend your time working on other stories, especially articles that can be pitched to friendly editors.

For a superb text on freelancing written from an *editor's* point of view, see *Magazine Writing: The Inside Angle*, by Art Spikol, Writer's Digest Books.

12 Advanced Article Marketing and Research

Let's assume that you're now a published freelancer. You have several articles to your credit, and your queries are eliciting more and more go-aheads. It's only understandable that, buoyed by this early success, you want to increase your sales and break into better markets. After all, your goal is not just to see your by-line in print—that's something you've already achieved. Now you want those by-lines to earn you a living as a freelance writer.

For this reason, you have to make sure your marketing and research strategies keep pace with your ever-expanding sales. If you adhere rigidly to the techniques that served you well when you were starting out, your once-promising career is liable to be short-lived, a victim of boom-and-bust. But if you maintain your early momentum and adapt new marketing and research strategies as your career progresses, you will hasten the day when you can quit your other job and devote yourself full time to writing magazine articles.

KEEPING ABREAST OF THE MARKETS

Despite the fact that *Writer's Market* is the freelancer's single most important marketing tool, this annually updated publication has one obvious limitation: it cannot reflect the up-to-the-minute status of the rapidly changing magazine marketplace. By the time

140

WM appears in the bookstores, some of the magazines listed are already defunct. What's more, the newest magazines are omitted entirely, since they may have come into being after the deadline for inclusion in the latest *WM*.

You should always make sure you own the most recent edition of *Writer's Market*. Buying a new edition each fall should become a ritual. But to keep abreast of the late-breaking developments in the magazine market, you should also consult a monthly supplement to *WM*. This supplement should be *Writer's Digest*.

First, a word about *WD*'s chief competitor, *The Writer*. Although I subscribed to *The Writer* for three years, I finally let my subscription lapse because, in my opinion, *The Writer* is a stodgy, conservative publication aimed primarily at the aspiring fiction writer. It provides very little nitty-gritty, how-to advice for freelancers concerned with nonfiction magazine writing, and only a modest amount of magazine market information.

Writer's Digest, on the other hand, offers its readers excellent information about current market developments. Three departments of the magazine are devoted solely to marketing: "The Markets," "New York Market Letter," and "L.A. Market Report." Here you will learn not only which magazines have died, but, more importantly, which have been born. These freelance-hungry, newly-emerging publications are profiled in great detail, often months before their listings appear in *Writer's Market*.

Writer's Digest also boasts "Nonfiction," a monthly column about magazine articles, written by Art Spikol, editor of *Philadelphia Magazine*. Spikol's columns are timely, thought-provoking, and a joy to read. Even if *WD* did *not* provide such excellent marketing information, "Nonfiction" alone would be worth the cost of a subscription.

But if you do subscribe to *Writer's Digest*, beware! Although many of *WD*'s feature articles are informative and well-researched, others are so lacking in substance that they're virtually worthless. (This isn't only my own opinion, either; I've heard several top editors voice the same complaint.) It seems ludicrous that a writing magazine would publish less-than-sterling articles, but a quick glance at the economics of writing for *WD* explains this apparent contradiction.

For years, *Writer's Digest* has been complaining about magazines that pay poorly, vociferously lambasting stingy publictaions. However, *WD* refuses to take its own advice: it still pays only 10 cents a word for its articles—the same payment offered in 1975. For this reason, *WD* is seldom able to attract the kind of writer who *should* be authoring its articles: the professional free-lancers who are writing for the top national publications.

This doesn't mean you should refuse to read an article merely because it appears in *Writer's Digest*. Just be selective. Before you read any piece, check the author's capsule biography, which appears in italics at the bottom of the article. If an article entitled "Breaking into Men's Magazines" is written by someone whose top credit is *Apparel Industry Magazine*, don't waste your time even skimming the piece. Bad advice can do more harm than no advice at all.

SPIN IT OFF, SPLIT IT UP

While reading *Parade* magazine one Sunday morning, I discovered an interesting piece of information in Lloyd Shearer's "Intelligence Report." Entitled "Beware of Lightning," this four-paragraph item told how lightning kills more people in the U.S. than floods, tornadoes, or hurricanes. One sentence in particular caught my eye: "Farmers, fishermen, cyclists, and golfers are frequent victims."

Convinced that lightning safety was an excellent subject for a magazine article, I queried *Farm Journal*, suggesting an article on how farmers can protect themselves from lightning. After receiving a go-ahead, I wrote the piece and it was accepted. Entitled "Lightning May Be on the Way," the article appeared in the magazine's March 1977 issue. Payment: $200.

Well, that took care of *farmers* and lightning. Still, Shearer's item convinced me there were other markets for the same story. So I queried *Outdoor Life*, suggesting a similar article aimed at fishermen and hunters. Again, I received a go-ahead and an acceptance. "Lightning Safety" appeared in the magazine's June 1977 "Field Guide" section. Payment: $500.

Then, temporarily, I put aside the lightning idea—after all, it was a seasonal piece. The greatest threat from lightning occurs during spring and summer, not winter. But early in 1978, I resurrected the suggestion and pitched the lightning safety idea to *Golf Journal*. Another go-ahead led to another acceptance, and "Warning: Lightning Is Dangerous to Your Health!" was published in the July 1978 issue. Payment: $250.

Unwilling to concede that I'd exhausted all the market possibilities, I also suggested the lightning safety idea to several boating and cycle publications, but to no avail. I was hardly disappointed by the rejections—after all, for me, lightning had struck not twice, but three times, increasing my earnings by a total of $950.

Quite obviously, my three lightning articles contained a considerable overlap of information. Still, each was unique, since each was aimed at a distinct group of readers. Although it is considered unethical to write the same article for two *competing* magazines (*Outdoor Life* wouldn't have been too happy if I had already written a lightning safety article for *Field & Stream*), there's nothing wrong with writing similar articles for noncompeting publications. In fact, such a strategy makes a great deal of sense.

If a previously published article can be slanted to other markets, consider writing a spin-off piece. Just be sure that you query a noncompeting publication and tailor the article to suit the needs of the new magazine's readership.

The adantages to the spin-off article are several. To begin with, it can save a great deal of research time. I acquired much of my information about lightning safety from the National Oceanic and Atmospheric Administration, and this information was incorporated into all three articles. Spin-off articles also help sell themselves. When I pitched the story idea to *Golf Journal*, I enclosed photocopies of the lightning stories that appeared in *Outdoor Life* and *Farm Journal*. This way, the editor was aware that I was familiar with the subject. Finally, because you don't have to start your research from scratch, spin-off articles can be lucrative: less time spent writing the spin-off piece translates into more time to pursue other article ventures.

Spin-off articles develop from stories that have already been published. But how can you achieve multiple sales if your original idea doesn't pan out in the first place? Try using the split-and-sell technique. Here's an example.

One day, while sitting in a restaurant having dinner with a friend, I came up with an idea for an article, which I called "The Games Airlines Play." The purpose of this how-to piece was to help air travelers better understand the rules involving air fares, oversales, delays, cancellations, and lost baggage. Convinced that the article had a high probability of being accepted, I began working on the query that same night.

At first the query elicited nothing but rejections. Finally, an editor at *Penthouse* said he would be interested in reviewing the piece "on spec." So I went ahead and wrote the article. A few weeks after I submitted it, the manuscript was returned with a form letter rejection slip. Although disappointed, I kept querying other magazines—and got more rejections. Finally, after more than a year had elapsed, I stopped querying. Give up, I told myself. It's a good idea, but it's simply not marketable.

Yet, just as I was about to consign the piece to my "Dead Article" file, I had another brainstorm. I was right: the article wasn't marketable—at least not in its present form. But "The Games Airlines Play" was actually five articles in one. Why not divide the piece and market each subheading as a complete article?

The strategy worked. Three out of the five subjects highlighted in "The Games Airlines Play" eventually were sold as full-fledged articles. *ASTA Travel News* bought stories about airline oversales and delayed flights. *Consumers Digest* bought a piece about finding the least expensive air fares. The split-and-sell technique had salvaged an otherwise unmarketable idea.

If you find that one of your ideas isn't marketable in its present form, try dividing the piece into its components and selling them separately. Of course, there's no guarantee split-and-sell will work with every dead-end idea. By their very nature, many articles simply defy division. But before you consign your own "unmarketable" ideas to the dead article bin, reread your query carefully. You might discover several *different* articles just waiting to be accepted and published.

AIMING FOR THE BIGGIES

At what point in your career should you begin querying the top-paying magazines? A lot depends on how long you've been writing and what kind of success you've had in selling articles to the middle-level publications.

In the fall of 1977, *Cosmopolitan* sent me a check for $1,250, the payment for an article about women in nontraditional aviation careers. That check marked a milestone in my career. Even though I'd already written for such national (yet middle-level) publications as *Psychology Today*, *Science Digest*, *New Times*, *Argosy*, and *Outdoor Life*, the women in aviation article was the first for which I earned over $1,000. At the time, I had been writing for two years, and I had twenty published articles to my credit.

This is not to suggest that *you* have to wait for two years and twenty articles before racking up a big-buck sale of your own. You may be able to break into the big leagues after only a year of writing. Then again, it may take you two or three years— even longer—before you achieve your first $1,000-plus sale. Such sales simply refuse to conform to any clear-cut timetable.

Although you can query the bigger publications at any point in your career, you'd probably do well to wait until you sell several articles to national, middle-level magazines. Not only will such credits ensure that your queries receive closer scrutiny, but the experience you gain writing such articles will prove invaluable once you begin to tackle the better-paying (and tougher) assignments.

One of the first steps to cracking the top-paying markets is to engage in a simple bit of self-promotion.

Whenever one of your articles appears in print, obtain as many tear sheets of the article as possible. In lieu of tear sheets, make at least a dozen photocopies of each article.

Tear sheets are the actual pages of the magazine on which your article appears. Some publications will send you several copies of the magazine when your article is published; others will send only one. In either case, if you need additional copies, ask your editor. He may not be able to fill your request, but it doesn't hurt to inquire. If you are able to get only a few tear sheets, then photocopy your article on a high-quality, dry-paper copier. Keep all copies of your articles in a special file folder labeled "Reprints."

These reprints serve a valuable purpose. Top editors are extremely reluctant to give assignments to relatively unknown freelancers. They're far more comfortable assigning stories to writers who boast an eyebrow-raising track record of published articles. If your query is accompanied by a tear sheet or a photocopy of a previously-published article, it not only alerts an editor to the fact that you *have* been published, but also provides him with a sample of your work.

Don't go overboard. No matter what magazine you query, you never want to deluge an editor with *everything* you've published. As a rule of thumb, three article samples is the maximum that should accompany any query. Just make sure you select those articles which display your research and writing skills to your best advantage.

One way to earn an assignment from a top-paying national magazine is to suggest a spin-off article. To pursue such a strategy, begin by listing several of the top magazines for which you would like to write. Then reread each of your published articles. Try to find an angle within those articles which might be marketable to one of the publications on your list.

For example, let's assume you wrote a piece for an airline's in-flight magazine, in which you profiled a 32-year-old woman who headed an extremely successful public relations firm. Perhaps you could pitch a story to one of the leading women's magazines in which you profile several successful female entrepreneurs, all of whom are under 35. Or what about a how-to for the women's mags? By interviewing a large number of female executives, you might be able to offer the reader some clues as to what traits are necessary for women to succeed in the highly competitive, male-dominated corporate environment.

Another strategy for breaking into the big-money markets is to build upon your area(s) of expertise. For example, if you've already written several health pieces for middle-level publications, then try suggesting a health article to some of the better-paying magazines. The topic doesn't necessarily have to be a spin-off of any of your previously published articles, either. As long as you have at least four or five health articles to your credit, you're well on your way to establishing yourself as an expert in the field. And you'll find that all editors—especially those who work for the top publications—prefer dealing with freelancers who boast some type of expertise.

Remember, though, that when you're pitching ideas to the top magazines, editors are going to be asking themselves one very important question: will this writer be able to produce the well-researched, well-written article he proposes in his query? Once you're established as a pro, much of this editorial skepticism will evaporate. Your track record alone will attest to the fact that you can handle just about any assignment. But until you reach pro status, you have to do everything possible to overcome the bias against rookie writers, so pervasive among top editors.

So when you finally decide to query the big magazines, take your time. Think your idea through carefully. Make several drafts of your query, and spend two, three, or four days writing it—as long as it takes to yield the best query possible. If appropriate for your subject, suggest possible sidebars for your article. (A sidebar is a brief story-within-a-story, usually boxed off alongside the main article.) Most importantly, be sure you have a thorough understanding of who reads the magazine and what type of editorial material is required.

The big-name magazines issue far less go-aheads than their middle-level counterparts. After all, thousands of aspirants are seeking just a handful of assignments. Yet, even if your initial queries *are* rejected—and the odds are they will be—you can still "score points" with editors *if* your queries are well-written and reflect a clear understanding of the magazines' readership and editorial needs. In fact, you may even get personalized rejections, in which you're encouraged to send them other ideas.

No matter how many rejections you earn from the top magazines, don't give up! Once you start to crack these markets, you'll find it becomes easier and easier to elicit go-aheads from other first-class publications. Selling to the biggies is a snowball-like process, in which one big sale can lead quickly to another and another. Making that initial big sale will depend as heavily upon your own persistence as on your marketing and writing skills.

KNOCKING ON EDITORS' DOORS

Another way to break into the top magazine markets is to pitch your ideas in person to individual editors. Since the vast majority of top publications are headquartered in New York City, such a strategy means you'll have to make a trip to Manhattan (unless, of course, you already live there).

But before you decide to book a seat on the next flight to the Big Apple, make sure your career has reached the point where such a pilgrimage will be worth the cost of the journey. And by all means, make it a point to "test the water" *before* you pick up your bags and head for the airport.

Never walk in on an editor unannounced. Always call or write beforehand to arrange an appointment. Some top editors are reluctant to meet with unknown writers, preferring to handle all communication via letter. Others are more than happy to sit down and chat briefly with a promising freelancer. But *no* editor is pleased to hear that Mary Freelance from Dubuque is sitting in the lobby, refusing to leave until she gets a chance to pitch her story ideas.

If you should decide that a visit to New York might further your writing career, then write ahead and sound out a few editors about the possibility of meeting with them. (Writing is better than phoning, since you don't want to put an editor on the spot in case he *doesn't* want to meet with you.) In your letter, introduce yourself by listing your credits. Enclose a few copies of your published articles. Mention that since you'll be visiting New York and you're anxious to write for the magazine, you'd like to drop by and discuss a few article ideas. Give the dates of your proposed visit, and enclose an SASE.

Should you receive enough positive responses to justify the cost of the trip, then go ahead and book your plane reservations. Just make sure you have at least one well-thought-out idea to present to each editor. Although you don't want to sound as if you're giving a speech, you should rehearse your presentation ahead of time so that you'll be able to give a concise summary of each idea.

Also, it helps to bring along a portfolio containing the best examples of your published pieces. To arrange such a portfolio, enclose each page of your articles in a plastic sheet protector. Then place the pages in a three-ring notebook. By flipping through such a portfolio, an editor can quickly get a feel for the kinds of stories you've written and what publications have bought them. Sometimes a portfolio can even lead to a sale.

During a trip to New York in 1977, I received permission to visit one of the editors at *Penthouse*. Shortly after we began talking, I mentioned that I had brought along a portfolio of some of my articles. The editor asked to see it. While flipping through the notebook, he spotted an article that I had written for *New Physician* on the ethics of medical experimentation. Suddenly, his face lit up. It seems *Penthouse* was looking for a freelancer to write a piece on behavioral modification programs in prisons. The *New Physician* article seemed to suggest that *I* was that writer. At the editor's suggestion, I wrote a query on the subject as soon as I returned home. That query eventually led to a go-ahead and an acceptance.

Keep in mind that even if you do get a chance to visit with some of the top New York editors, you're taking a gamble. Make a positive impression and, ultimately, you could land a well-paying assignment. However, if a face-to-face meeting with an editor makes you flustered and nervous, you risk making a poor impression, which could possibly destroy any chance you might have had for winning an article assignment.

Face-to-face writer/editor meetings are not a substitute for good queries; they're an adjunct. Unless you're reasonably confident you can enhance your sales prospects by visiting editors in New York, you might as well save your money and devote all your efforts to writing the best queries possible.

ON-SITE AND OUT-OF-TOWN RESEARCH

For many articles, research consists solely of collecting the facts and interviewing the experts. You may have to visit your local library, but often, such a visit is the extent of your "travel." As a contributing editor of *Frequent Flyer*, I find I can write most of my articles without ever leaving my office. Back issues of such magazines as *Aviation Week & Space Technology* provide me with vital background information. A phone call can elicit a pertinent report in the mail. And my telephone provides the crucial link with aviation experts all over the country.

However, depending upon the nature of the topic, some articles require more elaborate research techniques. A case in point was my Cook County Jail assignment for *Chicago* magazine.

As usual, I began my research by collecting as much printed data about the jail as possible. I spent hours reading back editions of Chicago newspapers, combing articles which had been written about the facility. I obtained reports about the jail that had been prepared by various citizens' groups and watchdog organizations. I interviewd representatives of the Illinois Prison and Jail Project, people who had firsthand knowledge of conditions within the institution.

But this research was merely preparation for the most important phase of my information-gathering process—an actual on-site visit of Cook County Jail. Obviously, jails don't provide daily tours to the public. This is one reason that conditions in jails are often so deplorable. Few "nonresidents" ever see what goes on behind those forbidding walls (not that many would jump at the chance, even if they *could* gain entry).

So what I needed to do was to find someone within the jail bureaucracy who could, quite literally, open a few doors. I found this person in the form of a staff member who worked for the director of the jail. After introducing myself over the phone, I outlined my requests. I not only wanted a general tour of the facility, but I also wanted to interview several inmates, as well as some of the guards and social workers employed at the jail. In addition, I requested a lengthy interview with the jail director, himself.

Thanks to my "advance man" in the director's office, my visit to Cook County Jail was extremely productive. I spent an entire day at the facility and was permitted access to all areas of the institution. I was even allowed to use a tape recorder during all my interviews, each of which was conducted in private.

No matter whether your research requires that you visit a jail, a hospital, an oil field, or an animal slaughterhouse, you have to locate your own "advance man."

Whenever your research requires an on-site visit, always enlist the aid of someone who can arrange your visit in advance. In most cases, this person will be a public relations executive. For example, if you wanted to visit Boeing's 747 production plant in Everett, Washington, you would begin by contacting someone in Boeing's public relations department. Tell the person who you are, what kind of assignment you're working on, and what you'd like to see. Give the date(s) you would like to visit, and leave a phone number where you can be reached.

If your research requires it, don't hesitate to "ask for the moon," either. After receiving the go-ahead from the men's magazine to write the article on chemical weapons, I became convinced that I could get a better understanding of the threat that stockpiling such weapons posed to civilians if I were able to visit one of several nerve gas storage sites here in the U.S.

A good idea, I thought, but totally impractical. After all, there was no way the army was ever going to let a freelance writer go prowling around a storage depot containing chemicals so toxic that a single drop can kill within minutes.

Still, I determined at least to *try* to arrange such a visit. I wrote a top-ranking public affairs officer at the Pentagon and outlined my assignment. Then I asked if I could visit the Tooele Army Depot in Utah, the country's largest nerve gas storage site. I figured I had nothing to lose by asking; all the army could do was say no. To prove that my request was legitimate, I gave my editor's name and phone number so that the officer could verify my assignment.

Much to my surprise, I received a letter back from the army consenting to my request. A few weeks later, I flew to Salt Lake

City, rented a car, and spent an entire day inspecting not only the storage facilities at Tooele, but also a newly built detoxification plant designed to dismantle aging nerve gas weapons. An entourage of army brass personally escorted me through my tour of the facility. Not surprisingly, my Tooele visit figured prominently in the article I finally wrote.

The moral of my experience at Tooele is, when in doubt, ask! Doors are opened far more easily for journalists than they are for the ordinary layman.

From the standpoint of logistics, the trip to Tooele was relatively easy to arrange. Once I received permission to visit the depot, all I did was have my travel agent book airline and hotel reservations, and reserve a rental car. The magazine picked up the tab for expenses, and the entire trip took less than forty-eight hours.

Other out-of-town assignments may require more elaborate planning. Consider the crime victim restitution story I wrote for the *Reader's Digest*.

After receiving a go-ahead and an expense advance, I had to decide which restitution programs to profile for my article. My goal was to highlight a few representative programs—five seemed a manageable number—located in different areas of the country. But the choice wasn't easy. A thick report obtained from the Law Enforcement Assistance Administration listed dozens of programs in all parts of the country. Some were relatively new programs; others were well-established. I couldn't possibly examine them all. Yet which to choose?

After two weeks of making extensive inquiries over the telephone, I finally selected five programs which I felt could provide the best examples of workable restitution: a project in Portland, Oregon, in which victims of crime are reimbursed by offenders; a program in Oakland, California, in which nonviolent offenders are sentenced to community service programs; an innovative program in Winona, Minnesota, in which a judge and an offender sit down together and agree upon an appropriate sentence; and two youth-offender restitution programs, one in Minneapolis, the other on Long Island. In each case, I was able to track down someone who arranged the details of my visit.

Of course, such extensive out-of-town research is seldom required except when you're writing for *the* top-paying publications. After all, such travel is expensive. Without a generous magazine reimbursing you for expenses, the research costs alone would eat up a large chunk of the payment for the article.

Should you receive such an assignment, be aware that *you* will be the one expected to arrange for the out-of-town research. In most cases, your editor will let *you* decide what locations you need to visit. Certainly, you'll want to keep your editor posted on your travel plans. And you'll also have to be able to justify the reason for your travel. If a magazine sends you from New York to California as part of your assignment, that trip had *better* be incorporated into your article. Otherwise, your editor could get the distinct impression that you were more interested in obtaining a free vacation than in conducting valid research.

To assist you in making airline, hotel, and car rental reservations, contact a local travel agent. There's no charge for such a service. Having a credit card or two in your wallet or purse will eliminate the need to carry large sums of cash. As long as you plan your travel carefully you'll have a hassle-free trip. And if you've done enough homework *before* you leave home, you can be reasonably sure you'll be able to obtain precisely the research information you need to write a saleable article.

3 | THE BUSINESS OF FREELANCING

13 Setting Up Your Own Office

I'm not very much of a morning person. To begin with, I hate waking up to the sounds of bells, buzzers, or those godawful electronic chirping swallows. What's more, I despise morning commutes. I abhor driving in rush-hour traffic, and invariably, the subway straphanger shoved next to me smells like he just bathed in a toxic chemical dump. I also loathe being friendly in the morning. What's there to smile about? For that matter, how *can* I smile? My face muscles don't even wake up till noon.

Fortunately, I'm in the right profession. Morning-hating freelance writers such as myself can avoid the prenoon hell obligatory for most other workers. Still, I share at least one experience in common with millions of other work-a-day Americans: I work in an office. Granted, my office bears little resemblance to those on Park Avenue or Wilshire Boulevard—among other things, I lack a secretary, a Xerox machine, and an in-house mail department to handle my postal needs.

But that's the tradeoff. What my office lacks in big-buck amenities, it makes up for in sheer individuality. After all, this is *my* office. Since I'm the only one who works here, I have complete control over how it's arranged and when it's used.

Once you're writing full time, your own home office may or may not bear any resemblance to mine. Every writer has different needs and different working habits. However, although your office may *appear* different from those of other writers, it should

157

still "work" as an office. It must be properly furnished, properly stocked, properly maintained, and properly organized in order for you to achieve a high level of productivity. Because high-output productivity is such an essential requirement for success, your goal should be to set up the most efficient office environment possible in which to conduct your research and your writing.

THE NO-FRILLS OFFICE

For now, let's assume you're just starting out as a freelancer. Obviously, before you begin to send out your first queries, you'll need to find a place in which to work. And before you decide what portion of your home or apartment you're going to set aside as your office area, make sure the location meets the following three requirements:

Your office area should be maintained in a permanent place. In order to be productive, you're going to have to be highly organized. However, such organization is well-nigh impossible to achieve in a now-you-see-it, now-you-don't office. So whatever area of your home or apartment you select for your office, make sure that area remains inviolate. No shifting the typewriter from room to room to clear a spot for dinner. No lugging the files from the basement to the attic every time the relatives drop by for weekend visits. There's too much instability in a freelancer's life as it is to tolerate such "If this is Tuesday, my office must be in the bedroom" displacement. Your office belongs in one location, seven days a week.

Your office area should be located where you won't be disturbed. If you live alone, this requirement should be relatively easy to meet. However, if you live with a roommate or with your family, achieving a measure of solitude can prove a formidable (but vital) task. After all, researching and writing magazine articles requires concentration. Unless you're a pro at tuning out the rest of the world, you'll be hard pressed to get much work done if your office area is located halfway between the kids' bedrooms and the kitchen. So if you live with others, you'd be wise to choose a spot as isolated and far-removed from the rest of the house or apartment as possible.

Your office area should be located in a room which has a telephone. As you'll quickly discover, a telephone is to a freelancer what a computer is to an airline reservations system—an absolutely essential tool. A great deal of the information for your articles— perhaps most of it—will be obtained over the phone. The telephone is also a key link between you and your editors. For these reasons, the telephone belongs *in* your office, not *near* it. You can't keep walking from room to room every time you have to make a business call. You can't keep putting your editor on hold every time you need to return to your office to search for an article file. So if a telephone isn't already installed in the area you select for your office, ask Ma Bell for an extension phone. Granted, you'll be charged an installation fee, and your monthly payments will rise a bit. But the additional cost is a small price to pay for an essential communication tool, linking your office to the rest of the world.

Whatever location you choose, remember: for now, anyway, your office doesn't have to occupy an entire room. If you already have a room available, fine—the more space, the better. But with your career still in its infancy, you can manage quite adequately with a small work area in the corner of a bedroom or a basement den. Just make sure your office is stocked with a few basic essentials, among them:

A desk and/or writing surface. A large desk is ideal. When you're done typing, you can push your typewriter into a corner and use the desk to review your research materials or revise your manuscript. A makeshift desk will serve the same purpose. Consider purchasing a sturdy piece of plywood and placing it atop two small file cabinets or other supports. Or you might want to use a kitchen or dining room table for a writing surface. Whatever you choose, just make sure it's flat and stable.

A chair. Old, new, expensive, cheap, stylish, or ugly. It doesn't make a bit of difference as long as you're comfortable, and you can see what you're typing.

Paper trays. To keep different kinds of paper sorted properly, visit your stationery store. You should be able to purchase interlocking plastic trays approximately three inches high. Stack four of these on top of each other and place them in a corner of your desk or writing surface. In the top tray, store your "el-cheapo" typing paper, the kind you use for rough drafts. In the second tray, place your letterhead stationery, in tray three, store your carbon manifolds, and in the fourth tray, keep the bond paper you use to type your final manscripts.

Odds-and-ends tray. This rectangular-shaped plastic tray comes with several compartments. Use it to store such hard-to-keep-track-of items as paper clips, rubber bands, stamps, and typewriter lift-off tabs.

File compartment. Once your career begins to accelerate, the number of legal-sized file folders you'll use will increase rapidly. If you don't own a metal filing cabinet, most stationery stores sell inexpensive 11 × 16 × 12-inch file storage boxes made of heavy-duty cardboard. Each unit is sold flat. Just follow the simple folding instructions, and before you know it, you'll have a sturdy and handy place to store your file folders.

Reference library. If you don't have a small bookcase in which to store your reference books, you can mount braces on a wall and use slabs of wood for shelves.

Lamp(s), a wastepaper basket, and a clock. How you arrange these items in your office area is up to you.

ONE ROOM, ONE WRITER

Like the author who works there, an office evolves with time. Just as a writer's career propels him into larger markets and increased sales, so, too, must a writer's office expand in order to provide room for the various writing-related furniture and materials that accrue with success. For this reason, a corner-of-the-bedroom office area, which worked well when you started out, will probably be inadequate once you begin writing full time. Turn pro and your office will probably have to occupy an entire room.

If your home or apartment lacks sufficient room for an office expansion, you may want to move to a more spacious place. Also, you might consider renting commercial office space, preferably in a location near your home. Another opinion is to find several writers or other self-employed professionals willing to share the cost of a common office. While neither arrangement is inexpensive, you may have to consider such alternatives if your home office area is no longer large enough for your needs.

For the moment, let's assume you *do* have a room in your home or apartment that you can convert into an office. What type of office layout is best suited to meet the needs of a full-time freelancer? That's difficult to say. There is no "right" layout. In order to give you some idea of how at least one writing office is arranged, I'll briefly describe my own.

When I first moved into my present four-room apartment, I converted what was normally the dining room into an office. Since the room is not large—just nine by twelve feet—I've tried to put this limited space to the best possible use.

In one corner of the office is my half-sized metal desk, which I purchased for $65 at a used office supply store. Two large drawers are built into the right-hand side of the desk. In the top drawer, I store a variety of personal and financial records. Since the bottom drawer is deeper, I use it to store manila envelopes and my typewriter ribbons. Above the leg opening of the desk is a wide, shallow drawer, with a paper punch, staples, labels, pens, pencils, and other assorted office miscellany. On top of the desk rest my typewriter, a high-intensity lamp, a four-compartment paper tray, an odds-and-ends tray, an ink pad, and a date stamp, as well as a manuscript easel on which I attach my rough drafts when I'm retyping my manuscripts.

Hanging from the wall beside my desk is a corkboard on which I fasten reminder notes. A nearby pole lamp provides adequate illumination while I'm typing.

Immediately adjacent to the left side of my desk is a 20 × 30-inch piece of wood, which rests atop a small table. This gives me a handy place to put a dictionary, research books, and other materials I may need to consult while I'm typing. It also provides a permanent location for my plastic filing tray (more about this item later in the chapter).

On the other side of this wooden slab is an ordinary dining room table draped with a plastic cloth. Since my typewriter occupies so much space on my desk, I use this table to go over my research and revise my manuscripts. A high-intensity lamp, digital clock, letter-opener, ruler, clipboard, steno notepads, and several pens are all stored permanently on this table. Because I'm constantly going back and forth between my desk and my writing table, I bought an office chair with wheels. Since the floor is carpeted, I can simply roll my way from one end of my office to the other without ever having to get out of the chair. (All right, I'm lazy—I admit it.)

Along the opposite wall of the room sit two 26 × 32-inch-high wooden storage units, each measuring 11 inches deep. Both were built by a carpenter friend of mine. I use one unit to store items such as telephone directories, frequently used reference books (*Writer's Market*, for example), boxed stationery, and the notebook portfolio containing my articles. The other unit is divided into sixteen equal-sized magazine storage compartments. *Time* is in one compartment, *Newsweek* in another, *Aviation Week* in a third, and so on. Since each compartment holds about thirty-five magazines, I have plenty of storage space for all my periodicals.

Resting atop these two units are the telephone, a small Rolodex address file, a cassette tape recorder, an answering machine, a storage rack for cassette tapes, a postal scale, and an office calculator. Anchored into the wall above both units are four rows of brace-supported book shelves. Finally, two four-drawer, legal-sized file cabinets stand side-by-side in the far corner of the room.

Although this office layout is ideal for my own needs, it may not be suitable for yours. That's for you to decide. At least now you're familiar with the way in which one full-time freelancer arranges his office. Just keep in mind that if you decide to convert a room of your home or apartment into an office, that room should contain only business furniture and be used only for business purposes, because in order to qualify for an important deduction on your income taxes, your home office is supposed to be used exclusively for writing (more on this subject in Chapter 16). Granted, the I.R.S. isn't going to send spies peeking into your windows to see if you're eating a peanut butter-and-jelly sandwich at your desk. However, if, for whatever reason, your tax return triggers an alarm in the I.R.S. computer, the agent who audits you may ask to inspect your office and see for himself whether it qualifies for the deduction. So a word to the wise.

Also, you should be aware that some local jurisdictions require self-employed professionals who work in their homes (that's you) to pay an annual business license fee. Ridiculous as it may seem, some jurisdictions even *prohibit* writers from working at home, insisting that if freelancers want to pursue their careers, they should rent space in an area zoned exclusively for business. Neither of these stupid, but onerous bureaucratic requirements may apply in your area, but you should check to make sure.

FIGHTING THE FEAR OF FILING

When I first began to write, I didn't pay very much attention to filing. I managed to keep the paperwork from my different articles in individual folders, but that was the extent of my organizational program. Why set up any kind of system when you only have eight or ten files in your whole office?

After a year, however, I discovered those eight or ten files had grown to over fifty. Still, I wasn't alarmed. I kept all my files in two neat stacks on top of a bookcase. Whenever I needed to locate one, I simply rummaged through each group, file by file. This nonsystem served me well—for a while, anyway.

Then one day, an editor called to verify a fact that I had included in an article.

"Just a minute," I said, confident I knew exactly where to locate the information. "I'll get my file."

Well, one minute turned into two, three, and four, and no matter how many times I flipped through those file stacks, I *still* couldn't locate the file I wanted. Greatly chagrined, I had to get back on the phone and concede defeat to my editor.

"I'm sorry," I said sheepishly, "but I can't seem to locate the file right now. Can I call you back?"

Fifteen minutes later, I not only discovered the missing file, but also four others, which I hadn't even realized were lost. All five had fallen behind the bookcase. "That's it," I said to myself. "I'm going to get organized if it kills me. From now on, I want to be able to locate any single piece of information within ninety seconds."

Did I keep my pledge? For the most part, yes. I've missed my ninety-second standard a few times, but on the whole, I'm far more organized today than I was when I first began writing. What's more, I'm determined to *stay* organized. I've found that good organization serves three very useful purposes. To begin with, it reduces tension. What can be more aggravating than knowing you filed a certain clipping and being unable to locate it? Second, organization saves time—and time is money when you're self-employed. And finally, good organization impresses editors no end. "What a pro! This guy was able to find that information in no time at all."

Now that I've given you three good reasons for being organized, here's how to get started:

The first step is one I've already mentioned twice so far in this book, yet it's so vitally important, it bears repeating once again:

Store every document, every sheet of paper pertaining to a particular article in a single file folder, and label that file with the appropriate title or subject.

If you're *really* an organization buff, you can go one step further and group the various materials *within* each file. Such extra work isn't really necessary, however. As long as you know that a particular file pertains to a single article, and as long as you know where to *locate* the file, you'll be able to put your finger on any information you need relatively quickly.

All your files should be kept in the same location. You can't leave file folders just lying around your office, even in nice neat stacks atop your bookcase. You need some sort of file compartment. The cardboard file boxes described earlier are excellent for this purpose, and they don't cost a great deal of money, either. But once you fill your third box, it's time to start thinking about buying a four-drawer legal-sized filing cabinet.

Whether you use cardboard boxes or file drawers, you should divide your files into three groups.

Label one compartment "Reference Files." Include individual files such as those assigned to queries, article ideas, university experts, routing logs, GAO Reports, *Writer's Digest* year-end indexes, and purchase receipts. These are just a few examples. You'll develop other reference files of your own. Just remember that the more highly specialized the file, the easier it will be for you to locate whatever it is you're looking for. Also, be sure to arrange these files in alphabetical order.

Label the second compartment "Subject Files." Here you should store all of your nonarticle files on various topical subjects. For example, because I specialize in aviation, I maintain several general files such as "Aircraft," "Airlines," "FAA," and "CAB." Whenever I need to locate background information for a particular aviation article, I always check the appropriate subject file first. Within this compartment, I also keep files on other topics in which I'm interested, such as gun control and American voting patterns. Although I have yet to write on these subjects, I hope to in the future. When I do, I'll have a head start on my research because each of these files is now stuffed with a great deal of useful information. Your subject files should also be arranged in alphabetical order.

Finally, label a third compartment—or as many more as you may need—"Article Files." This is where you store the files on all the articles you've had published, as well as the files on articles that were written but subsequently rejected. Keep the latter group stored in the back portion of the compartment. You may want to resurrect those stories one day or utilize some of the research information contained in the file. Then arrange your article files by the order in which the articles were published. The file of your very first published article should be located just in front of the "killed" files; the file of your most recently published article should appear toward the front of the compartment, directly behind your "active" article files.

Now that all your files are well organized, make sure you keep them that way.

Whenever you remove a file from a compartment, be sure to return it to its proper place. Rather obvious advice, to be sure, yet unless you *follow* this advice you risk sabotaging your whole filing system. Before long, you'll have files strewn all over your office again, and you'll be back to Square One, as disorganized as ever.

Items that need to be filed should be stored temporarily in a plastic "In" tray. Did you come across a newspaper article pertinent to the subject of one of your articles? Clip it out and toss it in the plastic tray. Did you just get back from shopping at the stationery store? Toss the receipt into the "In" tray. Did you finish typing three more queries? Make sure you place the copies of your queries in the plastic tray. Once or twice a week, spread the tray's contents across your desk and sort the various documents, deposting each in the appropriate file.

That's it. That's all you have to do to keep your files organized. Once these simple procedures become routine, you can boast of a home office that's every bit as efficient, as well organized as any on Park Avenue or Wilshire Boulevard.

14 The Mechanical Freelancer: Machines of Necessity

You begin the day in front of your typewriter. Having finally completed the last draft of your article, you type the final manuscript and mail it to your editor. After you're finished, you call a university professor who is helping you research another piece, and interview him over the phone. Instead of taking notes, you record the interview on your cassette tape recorder. While you're transcribing the tape, an editor phones and asks if you could photograph a nearby munitions plant to illustrate one of your articles. You agree. Flipping on your telephone answering machine, you grab your camera and head out the door to your photo assignment. When you return a few hours later, you check to see if any messages were left while you were away. Sure enough, another editor called, saying she's interested in one of your queries. Expectantly, you return the call and discuss the proposed article. An agreement is reached, and your day ends with an $850 assignment.

I relate this scenario for a reason. Although the above account is not necessarily a typical day in the life of a full-time freelance writer, it serves to illustrate how dependent freelancers can become on five machines: the typewriter, the telephone, the telephone answering machine, the tape recorder, and the camera. Although only the first two are absolute necessities, the other three machines also play an important role in the careers of most full-time freelance writers. Hence this chapter, devoted solely to a discussion of these five machines.

FINDING THE TYPEWRITER THAT'S RIGHT FOR YOU

When I began writing in 1975, I owned a $200 portable electric typewriter which, for reasons that will become obvious, I'll leave nameless. When the machine worked properly, it did a satisfactory job of typing—nothing exceptional, mind you, but passable, nonetheless. However, once I began to use the typewriter on a daily basis, my once-trusty little portable began—quite literally— to fall apart.

First the letter *n* broke off from its metal arm. Within a month, the letter *p* met the same fate. Eventually, *x* and *r* also succumbed. Since it's impossible to type an article without the letters *n*, *p*, *r*, or even *x*, I had to lug the machine to a typewriter repair service each time I lost another letter. Such repairs ran anywhere from $35 to $50 each. What's more, the drain on my pocketbook was only part of the aggravation. The repairs also resulted in reduced productivity. It usually took at least a week to have my typewriter serviced—a week in which I was without the one machine I needed in order to earn an income.

As I learned firsthand, most electric portables—even the much-ballyhooed name-brand models—simply are not built to withstand the continual punishment meted out by freelance writers. If you write your drafts in longhand and only use a typewriter for your final manuscript . . . well, that's another story and you may find a portable to be not only perfectly adequate for your needs, but also easy on your wallet. But if you use a typewriter at least once a day, then you should definitely consider purchasing a full-fledged office machine, which is designed to withstand the rigors of daily use.

You don't necessarily have to pay $1,000 for a brand-new typewriter, either. Factory reconditioned machines are available for about half the price of new models. Most are sold with a standard ninety-day warranty. With proper preventive maintenance they can provide years of useful service.

Regardless of whether you purchase a new or used office typewriter, you'll find that different machines offer different features. Among the most important for a freelancer:

A single-element typeball. First introduced by IBM in 1961, the typeball eliminates the possiblity that individual letters will, after a time, go hurtling off into space. This feature also permits you to use interchangeable elements for different typefaces.

A self-correcting feature. No matter how proficient your typing skills may be, you're going to make mistakes. This feature permits you to correct mistakes easily with professional-looking results. You'll pay more money for a self-correcting typewriter, especially if it boasts the more efficient dual-correcting mechanism (as opposed to a single-correcting devise). But if you can afford it, then by all means, buy it. You'll never regret your decision.

Interchangeable ribbons. Although even some top-of-the-line office typewriters will not allow you to switch back and forth between cloth and carbon ribbons, this feature can save you considerable money in the long run. Because cloth ribbons are relatively inexpensive and can be used over and over again, they're perfectly adequate for typing rough drafts. Although more expensive, carbon ribbons give that clean, professional look that's ideal for final drafts. Being able to switch from one ribbon cartridge to another gives you the best of both worlds.

Obviously, there are a great many other factors you need to consider when purchasing a high-cost item such as an office typewriter. So before you begin shopping for your own machine, you might want to read an article by Ronald John Donovan entitled "A Writer's Guide to Typewriters," which appeared in the January 1981 issue of *Writer's Digest*. This article provides a thorough, easy-to-understand discussion of what to look for when purchasing a typewriter.

Before you buy any typewriter—new *or* used—you should first consider renting the machine for a month or two. This way, you'll be able to learn firsthand what you do and don't like about the typewriter. In most cases, you'll be able to apply the rental cost toward the purchase price if you eventually decide to keep the machine.

You may also want to buy a service agreement—to protect yourself against costly repair bills. Although office typewriters are far more reliable than their portable counterparts, they're also more expensive to repair when they *do* break down and—let's face it—it happens to even the best of machines. In exchange for a flat yearly fee, most service agreements guarantee that the dealer will foot the bill for parts and labor if your typewriter should need repair. What's more, this wise investment is also tax-deductible.

Once your career is well-established, you might consider trading in your conventional office machine for one of the new-generation "smart" typewriters. In 1980, I finally parted with an Adler SE 1000 and purchased an IBM Electronic 75 with a ten-page (double-space) storage memory. This quasi word processor not only provides automatic carriage return, underlining, centering, and column layout but also features a one-step self-correcting system. Press one key and the typewriter instantly lifts off the previously typed letter. (Because it has an on-line memory, it knows exactly which letters have been typed.)

The 75's biggest advantage is its computer memory, which eliminates the need to retype rough drafts. Once the original draft is entered into the 75's memory, the text can be edited paragraph by paragraph, line by line, or word by word simply by pressing one of four special buttons. Assuming that all spelling and punctuation errors are corrected in the editing process, the machine will type an error-free manuscript at the press of a button.

Not surprisingly, the Electronic 75 is expensive. When I signed the purchase contract in August 1980, the selling price was $2,300. (In 1982, however, the price actually dropped to $1,950.) Although that's a lot of money to pay for one piece of office equipment, the Electronic 75 is one fantastic machine. Over the long run, the time I save in preparing my manuscripts will more than justify the steep price tag and the twenty-four monthly installments.

The next step up from a machine such as the Electronic 75 is a full-fledged word processor. The most sophisticated of these computer-age, text-editing machines consists of three separate units: a keyboard, a televisionlike cathode ray tube, and a printing unit. Whereas a "smart" typewriter such as the IBM 75 features an internal memory, a word processor uses magnetic disks that offer a removable memory. Such disks function much like the cassette cartidges used in tape recorders—each contains a certain amount of information that can be "plugged" into the word processor and displayed on the screen. Removable memory means that as long as you have enough disks, there is no limit to the storage capacity of your machine.

Like an electronic typewriter, a word processor permits a writer to edit a text word by word, line by line, or page by page. All editing is done on the cathode ray tube. And you can get a "hard" copy of the text by merely pressing the "print" button. Most word processors also boast an internal "dictionary" containing as many as fifty thousand of the most commonly used words. Misspell the word *conceive* and the machine automatically issues an alert, asking you whether you'd like to make a correction. You can even add your own words to the machine's built-in dictionary. In addition, word processors will "justify" right margins by automatically spacing the words so that the last word of each line of text ends at the same point on the page.

Because the machine costs so much, very few freelancers own their own word processors. (In 1981, the price for a full-fledged modular word processor ranged from $7,500 to more than $20,000.) However, it's more than likely that further technological advances in the field will eventually bring the cost down. So although a word processor may be out of your price range for the time being, it could become an affordable and extremely valuable writing tool in the not-too-distant future.

PHONE FACTS

Since you're going to be making plenty of business calls, you should make sure you have the most hassle-free telephone possible. So consider these tips:

● A touch-tone phone is clearly preferable to one with an old-style rotary dial. And a standard desk-top model is preferable to a trimline phone because the buttons are larger, and easier to press.

- Since you'll need a bit of freedom to move around your office without being disconnected, get a long expanding telephone cord that can be "clipped" between the base of your phone and the receiver. Electronic supply outlets like Radio Shack sell these spiral cords in varying lengths, and they're easy to install.
- To free your hands while you're on the phone, buy a plastic telephone cradle at a stationery store. Attached to the receiver, this handy device will permit you to rest the receiver between your shoulder and your chin.

To save money on your long-distance phone calls, remember that Ma Bell charges her highest rates on weekdays between 8:00 A.M. and 5:00 P.M., local time. Unfortunately, many of your business calls—probably the majority of them—will have to be made during those hours. But don't hesitate to use the time zone differences to your advantage. For example, if you live in the Eastern or Central time zones, wait until after 5:00 P.M. to make your business calls to the West Coast. On the other hand, if you're based west of the Rockies and you don't mind being an early bird, make your business calls to the East *before* 8:00 A.M.

If you find your long-distance phone charges averaging more than $25 per month, consider subscribing to a special long-distance service such as M.C.I. or Sprint. These firms compete with Ma Bell and generally charge cheaper rates, as long as you're willing to accept tradeoffs. For example, in addition to your long-distance charges, you'll also be billed a flat monthly fee, usually around $10. Also, such services will not permit you to dial every phone in the U.S., although you will be able to reach most phones in major metropolitan areas. In order to subscribe, you must have a touch-tone phone, and you must be willing to press twelve *extra* buttons before dialing each long-distance call (a local, seven-digit access number, and your five digit personal I.D. number).

Regardless of whether or not you use Ma Bell to make your long-distance calls, you should always keep track of all your out-of-town phone calls in a long-distance log book. (You'll find such logs available at most stationery stores.) Record the date, time, and phone number of each call, as well as the person you called. You'll need this record at tax time, since all nonreimbursable long-distance phone calls are deductible on your income taxes.

Finally, a word about telephone etiquette. Make sure your phone is answered in a businesslike manner, at least during weekday business hours. Don't have your 5-year-old daughter answer the phone during the day. Don't pick up the phone and say, "Yeah, whadda ya want?" And don't have your stereo playing so loudly in the background you can barely hear the caller. Editors are professionals. They assume they're calling another office, not a kindergarten, a union hall, or a disco. Proper phone etiquette is another indication of your professionalism.

IS THERE AN ANSWERING MACHINE IN YOUR FUTURE?

Despite the importance of the telephone to your career, you can't spend every waking moment sitting in your office waiting for the phone to ring. Of course, if you headed your own corporation, you'd have a secretary answer your phone. But since you're self-employed, you can hardly afford such a luxury. Even a spouse or roommate isn't always available to take phone messages while you're out of the office.

Editors and research contacts are hardly fools. If no one answers your phone on the first try, they'll generally call back later. However, some calls are more urgent than others, and demand a quick response. Miss such a call and you may have to forgo a valuable interview, or perhaps even a hastily assigned article.

An answering machine means you never miss a single phone call, business or otherwise. It means that no matter whether you're at the library, the grocery store, or the beach, you know who called (assuming the caller leaves a message, which most business callers do). In short, an answering machine takes the guesswork out of abandoning your telephone. No more, "I wonder whether Shifty Margin of *Trendy Topic* called while I was gone."

An answering machine also can offer you some much-needed privacy, as well. Since you work at home, chances are that at least some of your friends will assume you're free to chat during the middle of the day. If you are, fine, talk away. But there are other times when you don't want to be disturbed, even by your friends. Fortunately, most answering machines let you screen your phone calls. You'll be able to hear who's calling without the other party being aware you're actually in the office. If it's a business call, you can flip a switch and pick up the phone. If it's your best friend anxious to discuss his weekend exploits, you can return the call at a more convenient time. (Answering services perform the same function. However, such services are considerably more expensive.)

Don't run off and buy an answering machine the moment you decide you want to become a freelancer. Wait a while and see how your career is progressing before you make the investment. An answering machine isn't necessary for *every* freelancer. But if you decide you can put such a machine to good use, then check back issues of *Consumer Reports* for a detailed analysis of the features and costs of the various answering machines on the market. One option you should definitely consider is a remote device that will allow you to monitor your messages from another phone. This way, if you're out of town on another assignment, you can still keep in touch with your office by calling your home phone and retrieving your messages.

IN SEARCH OF THE CAPABLE CASSETTE RECORDER

Assuming I've already persuaded you that tape recording your interviews is infinitely preferable to taking notes, your next consideration is what kind of cassette tape recorder to buy. First a couple of don'ts:

Don't buy a micro-cassette tape recorder. Granted, they're extremely unobtrusive. In fact, these machines are so small, they'll easily slip inside your pocket or purse. Unfortunately, the relatively lackluster sound quality of most micro-recorders simply cannot justify their steep price tags. Another drawback is that you have to purchase costly micro-cassettes, which aren't even sold at most retail outlets.

Don't buy a large cassette tape recorder, either. The rule of thumb should be: if it has a handle, it's too large. In this category are the plastic-encased "bargain" cassette recorders, which sell for $20 to $40 at stores such as K-Mart. These machines are simply a waste of money. Not only are these recorders plagued by poor sound reproduction but they're also not built to withstand the type of punishment to which you'll likely be subjecting them. Of course, by increasing your cash outlay, you can purchase a similar-sized, but far more reliable cassette recorder. When it comes to interviewing with a tape recorder, bigger definitely is not better. You want your subject to confide in you. You don't want to intimidate him with a huge electronic gadget that resembles a prop from *Star Wars*.

Your best bet is to purchase a mini-cassette tape recorder. I own a Sony Cassette-Corder, which I bought for $75 in 1981. Although it won't fit into my pocket, the machine is still small enough—just 6 × 3 1/2 × 1 1/2 inches—that it doesn't intimidate the people I interview. In fact, after a while, most people forget it's even operating. What's more, it's extremely reliable. I've probably recorded a couple of hundred interviews on my Sony, and it's never once failed me.

Among the features you should look for when shopping for your own cassette recorder are:

An A/C adapter. Rather than draining your batteries, you'll be able to use your standard household current when you're transcribing or taping over the phone.

A battery-level indicator. Since dead batteries mean dead interviews, it helps to have some idea when your alkalines are beginning to wane.

A tape counter. By consulting this numerical monitoring device, you'll be able to quickly relocate a specific portion of your interview.

An end-of-the-tape indicator. Whenever the cassette in my Sony is nearing the end of a reel, a small red light begins to flash, warning me that my tape is about to run out.

Automatic shutoff. Nothing can be more aggravating than *thinking* your machine is still recording when it's not. This fail-safe device removes the guesswork. When your tape runs out—click—the machine shuts itself off.

Pause control. Extremely handy for transcribing, this option allows you to quickly stop and restart your tapes without pressing the "Stop" and "Play" buttons. Just make sure the pause control can lock automatically. You can't transcribe your tapes if you have one finger continually pressing the pause button.

Most mini-cassette recorders come equipped with a built-in microphone. Although such a feature is handy, the big drawback to a built-in mike is that it tends to pick up all sorts of extraneous noises, making transcription difficult and, at times, well-nigh impossible.

For this reason, I suggest you visit an electronics supply outlet and purchase an inexpensive hand-held microphone for about $15 to $25 (make sure the adapter plug will fit your machine's microphone jack). Since you're not going to be performing at the Hollywood Bowl, you don't need a large microphone. A 5- or 6-inch mike is ideal, and will immeasurably improve the quality of your recordings. You'll also need some sort of plastic, easel-style holder so you can prop the mike on a desk while you're interviewing.

Prices of mini-cassette tape recorders generally range from $60 to $200. Since competition in the field is keen, you should definitely visit several dealers to compare prices. Of course, before you buy any machine, you should first check *Consumer Reports* to see how the various models compare in terms of cost, quality, and features. Keep in mind that this is one item where a steep price tag doesn't necessarily mean a better product.

As for purchasing cassette tapes, don't bother buying the expensive brands. Although they're ideal for recording music, you'll be recording the spoken voice, not the *Brandenburg Concerto*. Therefore, you don't need to buy the highest quality tapes on the market. Instead, you can save yourself some money by buying the bargain brands that are made in Taiwan or the Philippines. I've used hundreds, and only one has snapped (and minor surgery salvaged that would-be disaster). Make sure you buy only tapes that provide thirty minutes of playing time on each side. You can find longer-playing cassettes, but to squeeze all that tape into the same cartridge, the tape has to be made thinner. Hence, it's more likely to snap.

GETTING A FOCUS ON CAMERAS

Why should a writer think about a camera?

As you can tell from even a casual reading of the magazine listings in *Writer's Market,* some publications won't even consider an article unless you can provide photographs to illustrate the text. Of course, you don't necessarily have to take these photos yourself. As discussed in Chapter 8, a freelancer can take advantage of a variety of different photo sources, most of which won't even charge for the use of their pictures.

Still, owning your own camera and knowing how to use it can be a big advantage to you professionally. Often, it's less hassle to take a photograph yourself than to try to track down an organization that can provide you with the same picture. And besides helping you market your articles, a camera can also increase your earnings.

When *Smithsonian* assigned me to write the article on earth-sheltered architecture, I traveled to New England and the Midwest to visit several underground dwellings. While on the road, I took along my 35mm Nikkormat and photographed every earth-sheltered building I visited. When I submitted my manuscript to my editor, I also enclosed my photographs. *Smithsonian* used five of my photos to illustrate the piece, and I earned an extra $600 in addition to the $875 payment for the article.

Remember, a camera isn't an essential tool for every freelancer. A lot depends upon your own area of specialization. If you write a great deal about economics or music, for example, you'll probably seldom need to take any photographs of your own. If, however, you specialize in a field such as travel writing, a camera is a must. So weigh your own needs carefully before deciding to buy.

Should you decide a camera will help your career and boost your sales, then you should purchase the kind of camera the pros use: a 35mm single-lens reflex. (Sorry, an Instamatic won't do!) Don't be frightened if a 35mm SLR seems too difficult to operate. Dozens of models are available which automatically measure the light and set the aperture. All you do is decide which shutter speed to use, focus, and then click the shutter. Before making any purchase, you should not only check *Consumer Reports*, but also look at back issues of the various photography magazines. Such publications regularly provide objective reviews of the various models on the market.

Once you decide which camera you want to buy, be sure to shop around for the best price. Since many discount supply outlets trim a substantial percentage off the list price, they can often undersell most retail camera stores. If you live in the New York City area or you're planning a trip to New York in the near future, then purchase your camera at one of the photo stores in midtown Manhattan. (Check the ads in the Sunday *New York Times*.) New York City may have a reputation for high prices, but when it comes to cameras, the Big Apple has some of the best bargains in the world. In fact, you may be able to save enough money to subsidize part of the cost of your trip.

If you're unfamiliar with the use of a 35mm camera, consider enrolling in a photography workshop. One of the best is the Nikon School of Photography, a traveling workshop that visits most major metropolitan areas at least twice a year. For a surprisingly reasonable price, Nikon offers a 12-hour course in 35mm technique aimed not only at the beginner, but also at the more knowledgeable amateur. You don't have to own a Nikon to enroll, nor will the instructor try to pitch the company's product line. Wisely, the Nikon folks have opted to teach, not hype. Even veteran camera buffs come away from the course convinced they've gotten their money's worth.

For schedule and cost information, write to Nikon, Inc., 623 Stewart Avenue, Garden City, NY 11530.

Who knows—you might develop such a fondness for your new camera that you decide to dabble in freelance photography as well as freelance writing.

15 Money Matters (A Lot!)

Like most writers, I love to daydream. In between assignments, I'll be out strolling through a park, when all of a sudden, I'll start wondering what it would be like to write without having to worry constantly about bringing in an income. I can just imagine myself sequestered on some sun-drenched tropical island, leisurely plucking away at the keyboard, working on the Great American Novel. In my dream, I never have to worry about money; as if by magic, all my material needs are taken care of. My only concern is writing *what* I want, *when* I want, and nothing else.

If only that dream could be translated into reality.

Such "if onlys" probably play a key role in the daydreams of most freelance writers. And little wonder. Unfortunately, such wouldn't-it-be-nice musings only make the brutal reality of our write-to-survive existence appear all the more cruel and unjust. After all, a writer is someone who is creative, talented. He's an artist, not just another laborer. He shouldn't *have* to worry about mundane, pedestrian matters such as the rent, the car payment, *and* the Visa bill when the checking account has been drained to just $200.

If only . . .

But no matter how unique we consider our professional skills to be, one stark fact continues to haunt us. Like every other member of the American workforce, we still have to earn a living

179

in order to survive. True, writing *is* an art—even writing magazine articles. But for the full-time freelancer, writing is, alas, a business, as well.

Hence, a chapter devoted solely to the subject of money.

THE TIME/MONEY EQUATION

What follows is a brief tale of two very different articles.

A few weeks after my article on behavior modification programs in prisons was accepted by the editors of *Penthouse*, I received a check in the mail for $2,000. When the check arrived, I was ecstatic—and for good reason. At the time, that was the highest payment I had ever received for a single article.

However, once the initial euphoria began to fade, I started wondering whether my financial bonanza was really all that much of a windfall after all. From start to finish, the prison story took two solid months to research and write. Ten days were spent on the road, visiting six different prisons and logging over seven thousand miles of travel. More than a month was required to complete the rest of my research, and it took an additional two weeks to actually write the five-thousand-word article. For all my effort, I netted an average of just $1,000 per month—hardly a windfall.

In 1979, on the other hand, *Travel & Leisure* assigned me to write a thousand-word profile of Washington National Airport. My research for this piece was thorough but hardly time-consuming. I obtained most of the information I needed during a four-hour visit to the airport. When I returned to the office, I placed a few brief phone calls, and my research was complete. Writing the piece also proved effortless. Since the format of the article was standard, all I had to do was organize my facts and arrange them in the proper order.

In all, the National Airport story required just two days to research and write. After the article was accepted, I received a check for $500. Assuming there are twenty-two business days in a typical month, this means that if I had written ten other *Travel & Leisure* airport profiles back-to-back, I would have earned *$5,500* for the month's efforts.

Which story earned me more money? Obviously, the *Penthouse* article. I received only one assignment from *Travel & Leisure* that month, not eleven.

Which story did I enjoy working on the most? The *Penthouse* piece, without a doubt. To this day, it remains one of the most challenging and fascinating assignments I have ever received.

Which story offered me the better credit? Once again, *Penthouse*. To be sure, *Travel & Leisure* is a first-class publication, but if I had to choose just one of these articles to send to another editor as a sample of my writings, the *Penthouse* piece would win hands down.

Still, the *Travel & Leisure* article had one important advantage over its *Penthouse* counterpart: it was more *cost-effective*. Hour-for-hour, I earned far more money writing the National Airport story than I did for the article on prisons.

The moral of this story is, *Once you've cracked the top markets and you've become established as a freelancer, you should always try to estimate how cost-effective an article will be before you accept the assignment.*

Certainly it's important to accept an assignment from a major national magazine when you're becoming established as a free-lancer. That's the reason I was so grateful for the *Penthouse* go-ahead. The assignment came at a time in my career when I was anxious to break into the big leagues. Even though the prison story was never published, I could still rightfully boast to other editors that I had written for one of the country's most competitive magazines.

Once you've *reached* the big leagues and you're attempting to support yourself full time on your writing earnings, the cost-effectiveness of an article should become an even more important concern than the amount of payment alone. For this reason, don't necessarily scoff at an assignment just because it pays a mere $200. If you can write that article in a day or two, and if your editor is so pleased with the piece that he doesn't ask for a revision, you've done quite well financially. By the same token, don't automatically pursue only the top-dollar assignments. Some may require more work than they're worth.

Of course, an article's cost-effectiveness shouldn't be the sole determinant of whether or not you accept the assignment. For a variety of reasons, there will be some stories and some magazines you'll be anxious to pursue—regardless of cost-effectiveness considerations. Besides, it's not always that easy to gauge in advance exactly how much time a particular article will require to research and write.

But since you're a freelancer in business for yourself, your time *is* money. So don't forget to link the two whenever you ponder the financial equation of any assignment.

EXPENSES AND INVOICES

Assuming that you're writing on assignment, rather than "on spec," most magazines will pay for at least minimal research expenses. Typically, these expenses will include the costs of items such as long-distance phone calls, photocopying, and research publications. Often, larger magazines are more generous, reimbursing you for research-related air travel, hotel lodging, car rentals, and business meals.

Each magazine has a different policy regarding expenses. *Whenever you're unsure how much money a magazine will pay for expenses or what type of expenses you are permitted to incur, call your editor and ask.*

For example, shortly after receiving my assignment from *Parade* to write the article on computer games and toys, I phoned my editor. Would it be all right, I asked, if I were to *purchase* a few of these electronic games? After all, if I'm going to write about them, I should at least be familiar with how they work. My editor agreed, but asked me to keep the cost below $200. Because of this understanding, there were no raised eyebrows in *Parade*'s accounting department when I billed the magazine for $172.45 worth of toys and games.

If a magazine places a ceiling of less than $500 on research expenses, chances are you will have to spend your own money to cover these costs. You'll be reimbursed by the magazine after you complete your assignment. Top national publications, on the other hand, will often agree to give you an advance on your expenses (provided, of course, that you ask). This way, you'll be spending *Trendy Topic*'s money on your research, not your own.

So don't hesitate to ask for an expense advance from the big-name magazines, especially if you estimate your expenses will amount to at least $500. Editors are well aware that few freelancers have large sums of extra cash just sitting in their savings accounts waiting to be tapped. Besides, even if you *do* have some extra bucks stashed away at First Freelance, why should you lose the interest on your savings just to foot the tab for *Trendy Topic?*

Regardless of whether you receive your expense money before or after you begin your research, you're still going to have to submit an invoice to your editor to document these expenditures. To familiarize you with the format, I've included a sample invoice on the next page. (For the purpose of illustration, I billed *Trendy Topic* for the article, as well as for research expenses.) When you're billing a magazine for expenses, be sure to photocopy the receipts of all your expenditures. Staple the photocopies to your letterhead, sign the invoice, and mail it to your editor.

If you've already received an advance on your expenses, the format of your invoice will be slightly different. Beneath the "Total" line, type the word "Advance:" and then the amount of research money that was forwarded to you by the magazine. Then type "Total Due:" on another line and add the two figures together. If the magazine still owes *you* money, the balance should appear as a positive sum. (For example, Total: $1,211.12; Advance: $1,000.00; Total Due: $211.12.) If, on the other hand, you owe the *magazine* money, a negative balance will result and a minus sign should appear in front of the figure. (For example, Total: $934.50; Advance: $1,000.00; Total Due: −$65.50.) If you did not spend all the expense money advanced to you, talk to your editor and find out whether you should send the magazine a

November 1, 1982

INVOICE

TRENDY TOPIC
1234 Fourth Ave.
New York, NY

Article:
    "The Great Midwest Water War"................$ 1,500.00

Expenses:
    Roundtrip Air Fare, Washington-Sioux Falls...   426.00
    Hotel Accomodations, Holiday Inn............   168.92
    Car Rental, Budget..........................   106.26
    Gas...   41.50
    Dinner at Spirits Restaurant with J. King....   52.79
    Long-Distance Phone Charges.................   61.33
    Book: <u>Vanishing Water</u>.......................   17.50
    Photocopying (35 copies @ 15¢)..............   5.25

                                       TOTAL: $ 2,379.55

David Martindale

check for the unused expenses or whether that sum will be deducted from the payment for your article.

Although most magazines initiate payment internally, some editors will ask you to invoice the magazine so they can process your article payment. If you receive such a request, use the same invoice format and bill the magazine for whatever fee you and your editor have agreed upon. If the magazine also owes you money for expenses, you can combine the article and expense charges on a single invoice.

One last thing about expenses: if you're writing on assignment and your article is "killed," you are still entitled to receive a reimbursement for your research expenses, provided that such expenses were covered by your original contract. For example, even though the men's magazine rejected my article on chemical warfare weapons, I was paid $400 for my research expenses *plus* the agreed-upon kill fee. As long as expenses are included as part of your contract, don't let an editor withhold your expense money merely because the article wasn't purchased.

STRUGGLING TO GET WHAT'S YOURS

In October 1976, *Argosy* informed me that it had accepted an article that I wrote entitled, "The Bizarre Deaths Following Kennedy's Murder." Since *Argosy* paid on publication, not acceptance, I knew it could be several months before I received my $400 payment.

Once the article appeared in the March issue, I began checking my mailbox a bit more diligently, confident my payment would soon arrive. Before long, the days turned into weeks, and the weeks into months. Still, the check from *Argosy* failed to materialize.

So I called the magazine's editor. After I explained the problem to him, he promised to look into the matter, but still no check. I called again, but was unable to speak with the editor. My messages went unreturned. I wrote letters to the magazine. That didn't work either.

Finally, after threatening legal action, I received a letter from an *Argosy* staff member on December 1, 1977—*nine months* after my article was published. In the letter, I was told the magazine's "cash flow crunch will remain tight. We do expect improvements in the new year." This was my first clear indication that the magazine was on the verge of financial collapse. The letter concluded, "I have checked my records for review during mid-January hoping that by that time, the obligation may be scheduled for resolution." Translated into plain English, I was being told, "Keep your shirt on. If you're lucky, we may get around to paying you in January. But don't count on it."

When I still hadn't received payment by *mid-February*, I decided that drastic action was needed. So on my next scheduled visit to New York in March, I stopped into *Argosy*'s office unannounced and asked to speak with the staff member who had written me the letter.

"He'll be right out," promised the cheerful receptionist.

She was wrong. Mr. "Check My Records" never did show up. In his place, he sent an elderly woman who I assumed worked in the accounting department.

"We owe you some money, is that right?" she asked. Obviously, I wasn't the first writer to plead in person for payment.

"That's right," I said.

"How much do we owe you?" she inquired.

"Four hundred dollars," I replied.

As soon as the woman disappeared from the lobby, I began kicking myself for being so honest. Why, David? Why? You could told her *eight* hundred dollars and she probably would have believed you. For all the hassle they've put you through, you *deserve* eight hundred dollars!

Five minutes later, Miss "Whadda We Owe Ya" returned to the lobby and handed me my check without saying a word. No apology. Nothing. Payment in hand, I left the lobby without saying good-bye, convinced that if I hadn't visited that office, I *never* would have received payment for my article.

That same year, I had a financial run-in with another magazine—the *Saturday Evening Post*. On August 31, 1978, an associate editor of the *Post* informed me that my article "Five Steps to a Longer Life" was not going to be published in the magazine as originally promised. But in a cover letter that accompanied the return of my manuscript, this editor said she was sending me a $100 kill fee.

Weeks passed and the payment never arrived. So I wrote her to inquire about the delay. She replied, "I've checked into this before and learned that there has been a check request made out for your $100. Since you have not yet received the payment, I now must find the weak link in our chain."

Obviously, the chain must have been far weaker than she ever imagined because the *Saturday Evening Post* never did pay me that $100. All further inquiries to the magazine were ignored. For a time, I thought of contacting an attorney, until I realized the legal fees would easily amount to several times the paltry sum in question. Small Claims Court was another option, but I was based in Washington; the magazine was based in Indianapolis.

Reluctantly, I gave up.

Why *didn't* the *Saturday Evening Post* pay me the money they promised? To this day, I haven't a clue. Perhaps the associate editor overstepped her bounds when she promised me that kill fee. Since the article had been written "on spec," the subject wasn't mentioned when the piece was originally accepted. Perhaps the *Post* was also strapped for cash. Perhaps someone in accounting didn't like the way I spelled my last name. At this point, it's anybody's guess.

Fortunately, *Argosy/Post* horror stories like these are relatively rare. The examples just cited are the exceptions, not the rule. Nevertheless, hassling with magazines to obtain payment is an occupational hazard of being a freelance writer. So don't be surprised if you find yourself embroiled in money hassles at least a few times each year.

How long should you wait for a check before you begin sending inquiries to the magazine?

As a general rule, if the magazine pays on acceptance, you have a right to expect payment within five weeks of formal acceptance. If the magazine pays on publication, you should be paid by the last day of the month that your article appeared in the magazine.

If a magazine is delinquent in paying you for your article, the cause can usually be traced to one of two factors: either someone forgot to requisition your payment, and the accounting department has no idea that the magazine owes you money; or, someone lost the invoice you sent. I've found that magazines seldom, if ever, discover these errors on their own. Editors are far too overworked to go back to the accounting department and make sure each freelancer is paid promptly—or for that matter, at all. Little wonder, then, that most magazines have no idea that payments are overdue until they're alerted to the fact by the writer.

So check your records. If you think your payment is overdue, call your editor and tell him. Try not to sound angry (which you may have a right to be) or panic-stricken (even if your rent *is* due within forty-eight hours). Just explain that you've been waiting for several weeks now and that you have yet to receive your payment. Ask your editor to check into the matter for you. Also, ask him to call you back and let you know what he finds out. If he fails to get back to you, be persistent and call him again. After all, the magazine did purchase your article. You're entitled to know when you can expect to receive the payment for that piece.

Hopefully, you'll never experience the *Argosy* nightmare of trying to extract funds from a dying publication. Hopefully, you'll also escape the "if we don't pay any attention to him, maybe he'll go away" stonewalling of a *Saturday Evening Post.* Yet sometime during your career—no doubt when you need the money the most—some magazine is going to drop the ball, and you're not going to be paid on time. When that happens, be prepared to be assertive. Otherwise you may *never* receive something you're entitled to take for granted—namely, payment for your services as a writer.

MEDICAL AND RETIREMENT COVERAGE

Being human, freelancers are occasionally afflicted with the same illnesses and injuries that plague the rest of the population. The inevitable result is medical bills, often large ones. As a general rule, employers offer their full-time workers some sort of medical coverage. Freelancers, however, can't rely on the largesse of an employer to protect them from financial ruin in the event of a catastrophic illness. For this reason, once you finally quit your other job and enter the writing profession full time, you'll be wise to begin shopping around for medical insurance.

Such insurance is never cheap. Individual medical policies are always more expensive than those available through an employer. A more reasonable alternative would be to join a health maintenance organization (H.M.O.). Under such a prepaid group program, you pay a flat monthly fee, which covers nearly all of your medical services. In many cases, H.M.O. coverage is less expensive than an individual policy with organizations like Blue Cross/Blue Shield. For a listing of H.M.O.s in your area, consult the Yellow Pages.

Another alternative is to join a writers organization, one that provides members with group medical insurance. (Such organizations are discussed in more detail in Chapter 17.) You'll have to pay an annual membership fee to join the group, but this fee can easily pay for itself if you end up saving a substantial sum on comprehensive medical insurance.

It's wise, also, to look ahead, and think about some kind of retirement plan. You might want to consider opening an individual retirement account (IRA). Under present laws, you're allowed to contribute up to $2,000 annually into an IRA, a sum which is deductible from your taxable income. In fact, even the interest and earnings on your IRA funds are exempt from taxes—at least until you retire and actually put the money into use. Best of all, you have a great deal of flexibility with an IRA. You don't have to contribute every year, nor do you have to deposit your money in any set increments.

When you're 59 1/2 years old, you can start taking money out of your IRA account, either in one lump sum or gradually, over a period of years. Should you become financially strapped before this age, you can also withdraw your funds. If you do so, however, you'll be subject to a 10 percent penalty, as well as a tax liability on the amount you withdraw. If, on the other hand, you only need a short-term loan, you can close your existing IRA account, use the money for as long as sixty days, and then reinvest the funds in another IRA. This way you can avoid paying tax on the money or incurring the 10 percent penalty.

Should you decide to set up an IRA, be sure to shop around. Various investment plans are now being offered not only by banks and savings and loans, but also by insurance companies, credit unions, mutual funds, and stockbrokers. All offer some variations on the IRA theme, so take the time to find out which plan is best for you.

OF BOOMS, BUSTS, AND BUDGETS

During September and October of 1979, I received $5,975 in writing income. Never before had I earned so much money in so little time. The boom was on.

Two months later, however, my financial picture turned gloomy. During November and December, I netted just $700. My boom had turned to bust—at least temporarily.

Unlike salaried employees, full-time freelance writers are no strangers to this feast-or-famine financial roller coaster. For this reason, budgeting on a freelancer's volatile income can prove as vexing as trying to unscramble a Rubik's Cube puzzle. After all, the very act of budgeting assumes at least a modicum of fiscal constancy. How can you budget when your income fluctuates more severely than the Dow Jones Industrial Average? The task is only compounded by the disparity in payment schedules among different magazines. Sure, you may know that several publications owe you $2,500, but a check promised is still a check uncashed. Until that check actually arrives in the mail, you don't know for certain *when* you'll be able to start drawing on those funds.

Still, if you're writing full time, you must at least *try* to budget, if for no other reason than to keep one step ahead of your creditors. Therefore, as best you can, itemize all your fixed monthly expenses: rent, food, car payment, and so forth. Use last year's tax records to compute averages for such variables as utilities and writing supply purchases. When you're done with your list, tack on an additional sum for spending money. Even a freelancer needs to splurge and take in a dinner and a show occasionally. The resulting total will give you a reasonably accurate idea of how much you need to earn from your writing each month to stay afloat.

Once you've begun to write full time, you're going to have to produce at least an equivalent dollar value of magazine articles to maintain your present life-style—as unextravagant as it may be. So use your monthly minimum expense budget to help you set financial goals for your writing. If you find that your earnings exceed your day-to-day expenditures, consider funneling a portion of the surplus into a savings account. At least this way, you'll have some cash handy in case that $2,000 article of yours isn't accepted after all.

Remember, the only predictable aspect of a freelancer's income is its unpredictability. Unless you have a ready reserve of cash, a single professional disappointment, such as a lost assignment, can easily trigger economic chaos. The disappointments you'll learn to weather are part of being a writer. But the financial havoc which can occur as a result is probably something you'll *never* get used to.

So plan ahead. Save for a rainy day. Even though you'll probably never encounter a full-fledged monsoon, a financial umbrella will come in handy during those inevitable thunderstorms that plague every writer's career.

16 The Tax Man Cometh

The art of taxation consists in so plucking the goose as to obtain the largest amount of feathers with the least possible amount of hissing.

J. B. COLBERT

Each spring, millions of American geese (taxpayers) fork over billions of feathers (hard-earned dollars) to one of the most notorious pluckers of all (the I.R.S.). That we hiss a bit in the process is not surprising. After all, getting plucked can be a painful experience, particularly for those of us who don't have all that many feathers to begin with.

Yet no matter how hard we hiss, taxes are still inevitable. Regardless of profession, every American who earns at least a minimum income is obligated to file a tax return by April 15. For many taxpayers, of course, this is a relatively simple procedure. All they have to do is take ten minutes to fill out a 1040A "short form," and their paperwork is complete.

Unfortunately, it's not that easy for us freelance writers. Instead, we have to submit at least two special "schedules" along with our full-length 1040s. Within those schedules, we have to tackle such accountant's mumbo-jumbo as depreciation, investment tax credits, and adjusted gross incomes. What's more, if we're earning even a pittance from our writing, we also have to mail the I.R.S. quarterly installments of our estimated taxes.

If all of this sounds so onerous you're considering hocking your typewriter to pay for entrance dues into the carpenters' union . . . well, take heart. Preparing your taxes doesn't have to be a nightmare. Nor do you necessarily have to head for H&R

Block just to find someone who can compute your tax obligation to the I.R.S. You *can* do it yourself. And once you get the hang of it, you'll find that your own careful tax preparation can yield healthy dividends. After all, the better you understand your tax obligation, the less likelihood that you'll have to pay those pluckers in Washington a single feather more than they're legally entitled to.

YOU AND YOUR RECORDS

In order to prepare your taxes properly and be eligible for every legitimate deduction, you must keep thorough records of all your business transactions. Such records are required by law.

As a self-employed businessperson, your chances of being audited by the I.R.S. are slightly higher than for salaried employees (more on this subject later in the chapter). For this reason, you must maintain adequate records that can be documented with appropriate verification (e.g., sales slips, cancelled checks, invoices). These records will not only keep you out of hot water with the feds, they'll also serve as a valuable barometer of how well your freelance writing business is prospering financially.

So here's what you should do. Visit any stationery store and purchase a four-column ledger book. On the first page write "Freelance Records" followed by the year. Then divide the book into three equal parts, and label each section as follows.

DEBIT/CREDIT JOURNAL
Use this portion of your ledger to keep track of your article payments. Above each of the four columns write the words "Due," "Paid," "Void," and "Net," in that order. Whenever you engage in any financial transaction with a magazine, log the date, the name of the publication, and the title of the assignment on the left side of the ledger. If a magazine also owes you expense money, list this item on a separate line.

In the "Due" column, list all writing income you expect to receive. (In order to avoid making corrections later, you should wait until your article has been finally accepted by your editor before recording this amount.) Under the heading "Paid," record all of the writing income you receive. List expense money on a

193

separate line and write "Exp" beside the figure. Use the "Void" column to rectify any discrepancy between the amount owed and the amount paid. The "Net" column will provide you with a running total of the writing income you have yet to receive. (A sample ledger sheet for each journal is illustrated on the following pages.)

Using this journal at tax time, all you have to do to determine your total yearly writing income is to add the sums listed in the "Paid" column (don't include your expense reimbursements in this amount).

OFFICE EXPENSE JOURNAL

In this portion of your ledger, list every single expenditure (except travel/entertainment) that you incur during the year. Include such items as stationery, typewriter ribbons, postage, and office equipment. Indicate the date of the purchase on the far left-hand side of the ledger, and then assign each expenditure a number. Cross-reference this number to your verification by marking it down on the appropriate receipt. This will allow you to easily match the two items at the end of the year.

Store all of your business receipts in a file folder labeled "198-Receipts." These materials don't have to be kept in any particular order. Just stuff them into your file, and sort them out at the end of the year.

BUSINESS APPOINTMENT JOURNAL

In order to deduct travel and entertainment expenses associated with doing business as a freelancer, you must keep a detailed listing of all your interviews, on-site visits, and appointments with editors and other businesspeople. However, this list should include only expenses you incur yourself, not those which will be reimbursed by a magazine. Entries should include the date, place, purpose, and cost of each trip, as well as the names of the people with whom you spoke. If you use your own automobile for business travel, be sure to log your mileage.

Once you establish these journals, update them regularly. You'll find that such accurate records will go a long way toward lessening your chore at tax filing time.

DEBIT / CREDIT JOURNAL   1982

	Date	Magazine - Assignment	Due	Paid	Void	Net
1	6/24	SCIENCE DIGEST - WINDMILLS	45000			
2	6/24	SCIENCE DIGEST - EXPENSES	4218			1717 74
3	7/2	HOUSE BEAUTIFUL - RESTORATIONS	35000			2067 74
4	7/7	FORD TIMES - YELLOWSTONE PK.		52500		1542 74
5	7/11	ELKS MAGAZINE HOME COMPUTERS	50000			
6	7/11	ELKS MAGAZINE - EXPENSES	2890			2071 64
7	7/14	USAIR MAGAZINE - INVESTMENTS		60000		
8	7/14	USAIR MAGAZINE - EXPENSES		4031 EXP		1431 33
9	7/20	MODERN MATURITY - BERMUDA	37500			1806 33
10	7/27	SCIENCE DIGEST - WINDMILLS		45000		
11	7/27	SCIENCE DIGEST - EXPENSES		4218 EXP		1314 15
12	8/3	OUTDOOR LIFE - CAMPING	50000			
13	8/3	OUTDOOR LIFE - EXPENSES	1704			1831 19
14	8/15	TRAVEL + LEISURE - LONDON	75000			2581 19
15	8/18	HOUSE BEAUTIFUL - RESTORATIONS			35000	
16	8/18	HOUSE BEAUTIFUL - RESTORATIONS	40000			
17	8/18	HOUSE BEAUTIFUL - RESTORATIONS		40000		2231 19
18	8/20	MADEMOISELLE - SURGERY	10000			
19	8/20	MADEMOISELLE - EXPENSES	6861			2999 80
20	8/22	FORD TIMES - EXPENSES		6025 EXP		2939 55
21	8/26	ELKS MAGAZINE - HOME COMPUTERS		50000		
22	8/26	ELKS MAGAZINE - EXPENSES		2890 EXP		2410 65
23	9/1	LOS ANGELES - AIRPORTS	65000			
24	9/1	LOS ANGELES - EXPENSES	4910			3109 75
25	9/5	MODERN MATURITY - BERMUDA		37500		2734 75
26	9/6	OUTDOOR LIFE - CAMPING		50000		
27	9/6	OUTDOOR LIFE - EXPENSES		1704 EXP		2217 71
28	9/10	PARADE - SENILITY	1200 00			
29	9/10	PARADE - EXPENSES	7581			3493 52
30	9/13	TRAVEL + LEISURE - LONDON		750 00		2743 52
31	9/13	POPULAR SCIENCE - NEW SSTS	45000			3193 52
32	9/19	SEVENTEEN - SHYNESS	1000 00			4193 52

OFFICE EXPENSE JOURNAL   1982

DATE	ITEM	Receipt No.	COST				TOTAL
4/20	LIQUID PAPER	25	1 29				126 65
4/27	PHOTOCOPYING	26	3 75				130 40
4/30	BOND PAPER	27	13 50				
4/30	CARBON MANIFOLDS	27	9 75				
4/30	ADDRESS LABELS	27	2 25				
4/30	RUBBER BANDS	27	1 10				157 00
5/10	LETTERHEAD - 200 SHEETS	28	23 80				
5/10	BUSINESS CARDS - 200	28	19 25				200 05
5/14	IBM TYPEWRITER RIBBONS	29	39 00				
5/14	IBM LIFT-OFF TAPE	29	28 15				267 20
5/18	BIC PENS	30	2 50				269 70
5/21	TYPEWRITER PAPER	31	4 20				
5/21	STENO NOTE PADS	31	2 00				275 90
5/26	FILE FOLDERS	32	16 50				
5/26	THREE-RING NOTEBOOK	32	3 75				296 15
6/4	PHOTOCOPYING	33	6 10				302 25
6/8	POSTAGE SCALE	34	11 50				313 75
6/13	BOOK: HAMMOND ALMANAC	35	4 95				318 70
6/18	TELEPHONE LOG BOOK	36	3 75				322 45
6/21	POSTAGE	37	24 00				346 45
6/30	OFFICE CHAIR	38	85 60				
6/30	OFFICE LAMP	38	32 50				464 55
7/3	PAPER CLIPS	39	1 20				
7/3	RULER	39	75				
7/3	BUSINESS ENVELOPES	39	11 20				477 70
7/11	STAPLER	40	4 50				482 20
7/20	EXPRESS MAIL	41	9 35				491 55
7/21	PHOTOCOPYING	42	5 20				496 75
7/25	ANSWERING MACHINE	43	225 00				721 75
7/31	MANILA ENVELOPES	44	12 90				734 65
8/1	TAPE CASSETTES	45	6 80				
8/1	BATTERIES	45	3 10				744 55

BUSINESS APPOINTMENT JOURNAL   1982

	Date	Item	Receipt No.	Cost		Total	Business Auto Mileage	Mileage to Date	
1	8/4	SUBWAY FARE TO/FROM LIBRARY		1 35		562 11			1
2		FOR RESEARCH ON SURVEYING							2
3	8/6	AUTO TRIP TO/FROM UNIV. OF					26	462	3
4		MARYLAND FOR INTERVIEW WITH							4
5		PROF. R. GLICK, ECONOMIST							5
6	8/10	ROUNDTRIP AIRFARE WASH.-NYC	26	118 00					6
7		TO MEET WITH AGENT ABOUT							7
8		BOOK PROPOSAL ON JETS							8
9	8/10	TAXI FARE TO AIRPORT	27	7 50					9
10	8/10	TAXI FARE FROM LAGUARDIA—	28	13 70		701 31			10
11		HOTEL BEAUMONT							11
12	8/12	HOTEL BEAUMONT, 2 NIGHTS	29	134 18					12
13	8/12	TAXI FARE FROM HOTEL—	30	14 20					13
14		LAGUARDIA							14
15	8/12	TAXI FARE FROM D.C.	31	7 50		857 19			15
16		AIRPORT — HOME							16
17	8/19	BUSINESS LUNCH WITH ROY	32	34 20		891 39			17
18		WILSON TO DISCUSS BOOK ON							18
19		JETS. PEKING DUCK RESTAURANT							19
20	8/29	AUTO TRIP TO/FROM ATLANTIC					375	837	20
21		CITY TO VISIT. L. ARNOLD							21
22		OF FAA TECHNICAL CENTER							22
23		FOR HELP IN RESEARCHING							23
24		SCIENCE DIGEST ARTICLE							24
25		ON AIR SAFETY							25
26	9/4	SUBWAY FARE TO/FROM LIBRARY		1 30		892 69			26
27		TO CHECK PERIODICAL GUIDE							27
28		FOR AIR SAFETY ARTICLES							28
29	9/11	BUSINESS DINNER WITH GLENN	33	41 96		934 65			29
30		JOHNSON. DISCUSSED AIR SAFETY							30
31		+ ROLE OF FAA AT LAROUE							31
32		RESTAURANT. FOR SCIENCE DIGEST							32

THE ABCs OF ESTIMATING TAXES

Although the deadline for filing individual tax returns is April 15, the I.R.S. doesn't like to wait until the tulips bud to receive their share of taxpayer earnings. That's why Uncle Sam withholds taxes from paychecks. However, if *Trendy Topic* pays you $1,000, the magazine will not withhold federal or state taxes from your check as it does with its staff members. Instead, *Trendy Topic* mails you a check for the full $1,000.

Before you laud the merits of such a payment policy, remember that in order to obtain at least some tax revenue before April 15, the I.R.S. requires most self-employed businesspeople (such as freelancers) to estimate and pay taxes on a quarterly basis. Unless your writing earnings are extremely meager, chances are you'll have to comply.

If your estimated yearly tax bite from your writing income is $100 or more, the law requires you to estimate your taxes on a quarterly basis.

This means that if you earn more than about $500 per year from writing, you're going to have to estimate your taxes and send the I.R.S. four quarterly payments. If your state levies its own income tax, this same procedure will probably apply.

Should you find that you must comply with this rule, obtain Form 1040-ES from your local I.R.S. office (contact your state tax office to obtain their estimated forms, as well). This form contains instructions, a worksheet, and four declaration vouchers. Read the instructions carefully and then, as best you can, estimate your total tax obligation for the year on the worksheet. If you're receiving income from another source—an office job, for example—and taxes are already being withheld from that income, be sure to subtract the withheld taxes from your total estimated tax bill. Also, if you later find that your taxes will be either significantly more or less than what you originally estimated, file an amended declaration. For details about this procedure, check the instructions included in your 1040-ES package.

Estimated tax declarations and payments must be filed by April 15, June 15, September 15, and January 15. However, if you file your year-end Form 1040 by February 1, you can skip your final estimate, provided you pay the balance of your tax bill when you file. Don't forget to estimate your state taxes also.

Remember—you cannot simply dismiss estimated taxes as a bothersome nuisance and hope Uncle Sam won't notice. If you ignore your estimated tax requirement, the I.R.S. may charge you a penalty—even if you pay your total tax bill in one lump sum by April 15. What's more, you may also be penalized if you do not pay *enough* estimated tax. By law, your total estimated payments should amount to at least 80 percent of your actual tax assessment. As long as you comply with the estimated tax requirements, you can avoid such weighty assessments.

FILING FOR FREELANCERS

Early every January, the I.R.S. sends its "customers" a booklet entitled "Federal Income Tax Forms." This package contains four of the forms you'll need to file your year-end return: Form 1040, Schedule C (Profit or Loss from Business or Profession), Form 4562 (Depreciation), and Schedule SE (Computation of Social Security Self-Employment Tax). The booklet also contains surprisingly lucid instructions on how to fill out each of these forms.

So when you're ready to prepare your taxes, here's what you do:

Begin with Schedule C. Fill out the information portion at the top of the form, and then record your total writing income on Line 1. Refer to your debit/credit journal to obtain this figure. (If you're also self-employed in a profession other than writing, you must fill out a separate Schedule C for each occupation.)

Now tackle depreciation on Form 4562. Although the I.R.S. does not permit you to deduct the total cost of major office equipment such as typewriters, tape recorders, desks, and chairs, you are permitted to depreciate the value of these high-cost items over the estimated life of the equipment. Instructions on how to compute depreciation are printed in your 1040 booklet.

Also, if, during the current tax year, you purchased any piece of business equipment which has a useful life of at least three years, you are eligible for an investment tax credit. This credit is deducted directly from your total tax bill and can vary from 3 1/3 to 10 percent of the total cost of the item. If you're eligible for this money-saving tax break, obtain Form 3468 and the appropriate instructions from the I.R.S.

All right, now go back to the front page of Schedule C and begin filling out Part II, which is labeled "Deductions." As long as you are seriously attempting to earn a profit as a freelancer, you are entitled to deduct the essential expenses of operating your business. However, if you incur nonreimbursable expenses while researching an article, such deductions may not exceed your payment for the article. Also, you cannot deduct research expenses until you actually receive payment for your article.

Although Schedule C lists twenty-five separate categories of deductions, only nine are generally applicable for freelance writers. These nine deductions are titled and listed in order as they appear in Schedule C. They include:

Car and truck expenses (Line 10). If you use your own automobile for business purposes, you are entitled to deduct 20 cents per mile for the first 15,000 miles and 11 cents for each mile over 15,000. Check your business appointment journal for your mileage figures.

Depreciation (Line 13). Obtain this figure from Line 5 of Form 4562.

Dues and publications (Line 14). If you belong to a writers organization or other professional group, you may deduct your dues. You may also deduct the purchase cost of a new book if it is intended for your research and you don't plan to use it again. Similarly, magazine subscriptions or single copies can be deducted if they are used for research or to analyze a market.

Legal and professional services (Line 20). Lawyers' fees are deductible if they result from some aspect of your business. Also, you may deduct the cost of professional courses and seminars, provided such training is aimed at improving your business skills, rather than teaching you *how* to become a writer (the I.R.S. feels that if you're truly serious about your business, you already *know* how to write). This category should also include deductions for such services as photocopying and professional typing.

Office supplies and postage (Line 21). Items such as stationery, file folders, envelopes, paper clips, and so forth qualify for this deduction. Consult your office expense journal.

Rent on business property (Line 23). If you use a portion of your home or apartment as your office, you may be entitled to deduct a percentage of your mortgage or rent on Schedule C. However, your office must meet a strict test.

To qualify for an office deduction, your home office must be your principal place of business and must be used exclusively for writing—no other purpose.

Do you eat all your meals at your desk? Do you store old clothes in your office closet? Do your kids use your office as a playroom on Saturday mornings? If so, you're ineligible for this deduction. According to the I.R.S., there should be a complete absence of nonbusiness furniture within your office. And writing is the *only* activity which should take place there.

If you pass this test, then compute your deduction as follows: Let's assume you pay $400 monthly rent for your four-room apartment. If so, you're entitled to deduct one-fourth of your rent on Schedule C (in this case, $1,200 for the year). A five-room house would mean a one-fifth deduction, and so on.

Repairs (Line 24). Deduct the cost of any repairs to office machinery, such as typewriters and answering machines.

Travel and entertainment (Line 27). This includes all air, rail, bus, mass transit, and taxi fares associated with your research or your other business endeavors. Also, include the costs of overnight lodging as well as any business meals. Obtain this information from your business appointment journal.

Utilities and telephone (Line 28). If you pass the home office test, then you are also eligible to deduct the same percentage of your utilities. For example, if you are permitted to deduct one-fourth of your rent, you're also entitled to deduct one-fourth of your utility bills.

If you have a separate telephone line used exclusively for business, then you may deduct the total cost of that phone service. However, if you use the same phone for both business and personal calls, deduct only nonreimbursable long-distance business calls.

After listing each of your deductions on the appropriate line in Part II of Schedule C, add them together and record the figure on Line 32. Then subtract the total dollar value of your deductions from your gross receipts and record the balance on Line 33. This final figure is either your net profit or your net loss from your business.

Provided you show a net profit of at least $400, your next step is to fill out Schedule SE. This form is used to compute the amount of money you must contribute to Social Security. Called a self-employment tax, this levy is assessed at a rate of 9.3 percent on the first $29,700 of your income. To compute the tax, simply record your net profit from Schedule C on Lines 5a, 6, 8, 12b, and 13. Then complete the rest of the form as instructed. The amount of self-employment tax you owe will be recorded on Line 18 of Schedule SE.

Now, at long last, you're ready to fill out your 1040 form. (Although the following discussion is limited primarily to your writing-related income, credits, and taxes, don't forget to also compute any nonwriting credits or deductions to which you are entitled.) Begin by listing your net income or loss from Schedule C on Line 11 of your 1040. If you earned nonwriting wages in addition to your writing income, include this figure in Line 7, and then complete the rest of the page. Turn the form over and complete the tax computation section. Record your investment tax credit (if any) on Line 41, your self-employment tax on Line 48, and the amount you paid in estimated taxes on Line 56. Complete your computations to determine whether you owe the I.R.S.—or the I.R.S. owes you.

If you find that you've overpaid your taxes, you should consider applying that balance toward your first quarterly payment of the new year's estimated taxes. (This first payment is also due on April 15.) If, on the other hand, you owe the government additional tax payments, you'll have to mail your payment with your 1040 and appropriate schedules. (Do not mail the receipts that substantiate your deductions. Such verification is needed only if you are audited.)

If you find yourself strapped for cash on April 15, don't wait to file your return until you have the money. Instead, file on time, and pay as much of your tax bill as possible. The I.R.S. will send you a bill for the balance, which will include an interest charge and possibly a failure-to-pay penalty. This assessment is much lower than the one levied on late returns. For unless you file your return by April 15, the I.R.S. will charge you a 5 percent penalty for each *month* your return is late (not to exceed 25 percent of your taxes).

Should you need assistance in computing your taxes, contact a lawyer, accountant, professional tax preparer, or the I.R.S.

Finally, a brief word about state and local income taxes. If your state or city levies an income tax, you'll find that the filing forms—1040, Schedule C, etc.—are fairly similar to those of the I.R.S. Use your federal forms as a guide. However, you will not have to fill out state or local Schedule SEs, since only the federal government can levy taxes for Social Security. Always complete your federal forms first, then your state or local returns.

OF AUTHORS AND AUDITS

Because so many self-employed taxpayers keep poor financial records or claim imaginative deductions, the tax return of a freelance writer stands a greater chance of being audited than one filed by a wage-earning employee with a comparable income. If you are sincere about your freelance career, and if you have shown a profit on Schedule C, you shouldn't panic if the I.R.S. notifies you that it's auditing your return. In most cases, the agency will not go over each and every entry with a fine-tooth comb. Instead, you'll be notified specifically which portions of your return the I.R.S. would like to verify (travel and entertainment expenses, for example). Hence, the requirement to keep complete records and verification of your expenses.

To prepare yourself for an audit, you might want to go back and read some of the newspaper and magazine articles already written on the subject. A quick glance through the *Reader's Guide* and you're bound to find at least a few "How to Survive an Audit" articles recent enough to be helpful.

Don't be surprised if the I.R.S. questions the sincerity of your writing effort. According to the agency, "doing business" is defined as "the regular pursuit of an income." For this reason, the feds take a dim view of anyone who dabbles in writing merely as a ploy to obtain tax deductions. The I.R.S. wants to be assured that you're serious about your career as a freelancer. So if you *are* audited, you might have to prove to the I.R.S. that you're not just a writing "hobbyist." In other words, you might be asked to provide tangible evidence that writing is, in fact, your business—evidence such as letterhead stationery, business cards, a business phone, rejection slips, membership in a writers' organization, and, of course, copies of published articles.

The I.R.S. also wants you to make a profit at your business. After all, the more money you earn, the more the government can collect. So if the I.R.S. learns you haven't been able to show a profit on Schedule C for at least two out of the last five years, they may question whether your career is a legitimate one. In fact, if your expenses exceed your writing income for three years in a row, the I.R.S. insists that, during that third year, you list your writing income on Line 20 under "Other Income," thus making you ineligible for claiming deductions on Schedule C.

In most cases, if your tax return hasn't been audited within three years of the filing date, you're unlikely to be called on the carpet by the I.R.S. Still, you should keep all of your financial records for at least seven years, longer if possible. Certainly they'll come in handy if you ever want to obtain a home mortgage (without such records, your bank has no way of verifying your income). Just be sure to segregate your financial records by year. Designate a separate file for each year's taxes, and deposit your receipts, copies of your tax forms, and your ledger journals in the appropriate folders.

And while you're thinking about taxes, you might also want to consider opening up a special savings account to cover your tax costs. A certain sum set aside from your earnings each month can lessen the financial bite at tax time. Such a savings account will permit you to earn an interest bonus, as well—a bonus which is not taxable by the I.R.S. unless it exceeds $400.

A word of caution: although I've tried to ensure the accuracy of this tax information, this chapter has not been officially approved by the I.R.S. Also, since the tax laws change periodically, be sure to read your tax instructions thoroughly before submitting any forms.

17 Broadening Your Scope

For the last sixteen chapters, I've been talking about one subject: how to pursue a career writing magazine articles. Hopefully, you now know a *lot* more about this topic than you did when you began to read this book. And hopefully, you'll be able to put this information to work, rack up a string of impressive article sales, and join the ranks of the full-time freelancers.

Clearly, writing magazine articles offers an excellent opportunity—perhaps the best chance of all—for the would-be author to break into the writing field and establish a name for himself. Yet having articles published in magazines—even the top national publications—is seldom an end in itself. More often than not, it's merely the first port of call in a life-long professional journey. For once you achieve a measure of success in the magazine field, you'll probably grow restless after a while and decide to expand your career horizons, staking your claim to other writing endeavors.

Widening your professional scope isn't always easy. Even if you've written more than a hundred magazine articles, it doesn't mean that a publisher will automatically agree to publish your novel, or that a Broadway producer will leap at the chance to stage your play. Skill in one area of writing doesn't necessarily translate to other areas of the profession. Nevertheless, the fact that you *are* a published writer is definitely to your advantage. What you do with this advantage—what other writing avenues you may choose to pursue—is entirely up to you.

JOINING A WRITER'S GROUP

One way to expand your professional horizons is to join a writer's organization. Some of these groups consist primarily of locally based freelancers. Examples are the Washington Independent Writers Association, Inc., and the Independent Writers of Chicago. Others are national organizations, for example, the Authors Guild, Inc., and the National Writers Club, Inc. And some writer's organizations are comprised solely of journalists who specialize in writing about particular subjects, for example, the Football Writers Association of America and the Society of American Travel Writers.

Such groups often offer their members a number of useful services. Among them:

A monthly newsletter. Besides keeping members informed of upcoming events and activities, newsletters also provide valuable market information for freelancers.

Inclusion in a membership directory. Typically, the organization will distribute this directory to publications or groups that regularly contract the services of freelance journalists. By providing a respectable advertising forum, the organization is able to help a writer market his expertise to those who may be in need of his services.

Professional seminars and workshops. Covering a wide range of writing-related topics, such educational forums are usually offered free of charge to members.

Group health insurance. A health plan organized under the auspices of a writer's organization is usually cheaper than an individual health policy.

Job referral banks. This service alerts writers to corporate and professional clients who are seeking the services of freelancers.

Legal advice and/or legal insurance.

Social functions.

Contests and grants.

In most cases, a writer's organization will grant active member status only to those writers who meet certain publication requirements (for example, the sale of at least three magazine articles). Often, however, associate membership is available to anyone with a serious interest in the profession. Although yearly dues vary anywhere from $5 to $100, most organizations charge $40 or less. Some groups also levy a one-time-only initiation fee.

Should you decide that you might like to join a writers group, check the index in *Writer's Market* under the heading "Writer's Organizations." If you spot a group that interests you, write and ask for more information. As long as a writer's organization offers services which you can use, and as long as you can afford the dues, you should join—at least for a year.

There's a good chance the market information alone will be worth the cost of membership. Besides, the dues are deductible from your income taxes. And if, after a year's trial, you feel the advantages of membership aren't worth the cost, you can always bow out.

BEYOND MAGAZINE ARTICLES

After you become established as a full-time freelancer, you may want to supplement your income from magazine articles by engaging in any one of a number of writing-related projects. This is one reason why membership in a writer's organization—particularly a locally based group—is so important. By acting as a conduit between freelancers and corporate/professional executives, these organizations can help you generate additional writing income.

Besides magazine articles, the most common writing projects for freelancers include:

Brochures. Many businesses and public relations firms hire freelancers to research and write such publications.

Slide, tape, and film scripts. Both independent producers, as well as large corporations, frequently employ freelancers to prepare audiovisual presentations.

Advertising copy. Sometimes the work is seasonal; other times, permanent. Rates can range as high as $50 per day.

Ghostwriting trade journal articles. The axiom "publish or perish" is true not only in academia, but also in a large segment of the corporate world. Since many professionals are often embarrassed by their poor writing skills, they team up with freelancers for assistance in preparing their articles.

Speechwriting for executives and politicians. You don't think the president of Murray Hill Electronics and the mayor of Canoga Falls write their own speeches, do you? Freelancers often pen those speeches for them.

These are just a few examples of how you can supplement your magazine income. For a detailed listing of dozens of income-producing writing projects, check the section in *Writer's Market* entitled "How Much Should I Charge?" Besides listing a wide range of writing ventures, *WM* also provides a rough estimate of what to charge. If you would like more information on how to bill business clients for writing projects, you should obtain "The ABWA Pay Formula," a computation method for figuring fair payment. To obtain a copy, write to The Associated Business Writers of America, P.O. Box 135, Monmouth Junction, NJ 08852. Two other sources of writing projects include selected articles in *Writer's Digest* (once again, check the author's credentials), and *Jobs for Writers*, a Writer's Digest Book edited by Kirk Polking.

Who knows? Once you've been writing magazine articles for a while, you may just decide to chuck the freelance life-style and take a staff job with a magazine. Should you opt to work on the other side of the fence, you can either wait for a magazine to approach you with an unsolicited offer—it happens, although rarely—or you can send out a few feelers of your own.

Generally, lower- and middle-level publications offer the best opportunities for employment, although salaries are often meager. If you target a specific magazine and you already know one of the editors, you might think about subtly raising the subject of possible employment during one of your conversations. If such an approach proves futile, your only other alternative is to prepare a resume, send it out to a number of magazines, and see what kind of responses it draws. In the meantime, you can continue your career as a freelancer and keep your fingers crossed that a friendly editor will tip you off to an editorial job opening.

OF AUTHORS AND AGENTS

Eventually, most full-time freelancers reach the point in their careers where they consider writing a book. The advantages of writing books are several. To begin with, a book provides an author with a certain measure of prestige. It's one thing to see your by-line on a magazine article. It's quite another to have your name appear on a book jacket. If a reader buys a magazine in which your by-line appears, he seldom selects that magazine just to read your particular article. But if he buys your book . . . well, that's a different story. Then he's purchasing something written solely by you.

Books can also be far more lucrative than magazine articles. To be sure, the vast majority of titles fall far short of soaring to the ranks of best-sellers. Still, a book can earn you not only an advance, but also royalties. Write a magazine article and you receive a fixed payment, regardless of how many issues the magazine sells. Write a book and you may end up generating royalty checks—albeit modest ones—for five or ten years, even longer.

Just as one article can be spun off to generate another, so too, can a magazine article provide the basis for a nonfiction book, even a novel. My first book, *Earth Shelters*, was a direct outgrowth of my earth-sheltered architecture article that appeared in *Smithsonian*. The fact that I was already knowledgable on the subject was certainly a factor in securing a contract from the publisher. So once your career is well established and you decide you'd like to write a book, go back and reread your published articles. You may find that one of your stories is an obvious candidate for a full-length book.

Regardless of whether you want to write a nonfiction book or a novel, you should never try to market a book alone.

If you have an idea for a book, don't query publishers directly. Get yourself a literary agent. Marketing a book is considerably tougher than selling your own magazine articles. Market it yourself and you'll be at the mercy of publishers who, while they're not out to rip off their authors, *are* out to maximize their profits. A reputable literary agent, on the other hand, knows the ins and outs of book marketing. That's his job. Unlike you, an agent has clout with publishers. He can drive a far tougher bargain than you, and can almost always negotiate a far better contract for you than you could ever hope to win on your own.

Most literary agents are based in New York City, and although some now receive 15 percent commissions, most still charge 10 percent. Because 10 percent of $500—even $1,000—is a relatively small sum, most agents do not market magazine articles. Nor should you expect them to. You're far better off doing your own article marketing. This way, you'll be able to keep your fingers on the pulse of the magazine market. Besides, an agent-sponsored article won't necessarily give you an edge on the competition. If an article is unsuitable for publication, it's going to be rejected—agent or no agent.

For obvious reasons, most agents are reluctant to take on writers who have little or no previous writing experience. If you have a book idea but you've only been writing magazine articles for a short time, put your idea on hold and wait a while before trying to locate an agent.

First things first. Before you try to break into the highly competitive field of book publishing, you're far better off working toward getting yourself established as a magazine journalist. By all means, branch out—once your career is established. But until then, stick with articles. In the long run, such a career strategy will pay the best dividends.

Why? Because if you work hard and develop a good reputation as a promising writer, you may not even *have* to go looking for an agent—an agent or publisher may come looking for you. This is how I met my own agent. While talking with an editor of a women's magazine, the agent who now represents me mentioned that she was looking for a writer to do a certain book. As luck would have it, the editor was someone I knew and had written for frequently. She suggested that the agent contact me. And even though I declined to write the book she proposed, my agent and I went on to establish a professional relationship—one that now includes two books and, hopefully, several more in the future.

If an agent doesn't come to you, then your first step in securing representation is to obtain lists of reputable literary agents. Such lists are available from two organizations; The Society of Authors' Representatives, 40 E. 49th Street, New York, NY 10016; and The Independent Literary Agents Association, Box 5257, FDR Station, New York, NY 10022. Enclose SASEs and request the membership lists of both organizations.

When you decide which agent(s) to contact, don't send an entire book or even a lengthy outline. Do the same thing you would do if you were proposing a story to a magazine—query first. Introduce yourself by mentioning your writing background and your magazine credits. Enclose one or two copies of your best published articles. Then *briefly* outline your book idea. Enclose an SASE, and wait a few weeks for a response before contacting another agent. As long as your credentials are solid and your idea is a marketable one, you can rest assured you'll find an agent who is eager to represent you.

(For a more thorough discussion of this subject, be sure to read Diane Cleaver's article "All About Agents" in the June 1980 issue of *Writer's Digest*. Ms. Cleaver is an agent herself, and her superb article touches on just about every aspect of the author/agent relationship.)

WHAT NEXT FOR YOUR CAREER?

A book, a novel, a play, an editorial staff job—all of these ventures or none of them—could be a part of your writing future. A hallmark of the freelance writing profession is that a writer never knows exactly where his career is taking him. This can lead to some troubling insecurities, to be sure. But the lack of a clear-cut road map can also be downright exciting. In fact, as your career progresses, you'll probably begin comparing it to a mystery novel: you know what has happened already; you know what *might* happen in the future; yet you're still unsure exactly how it's all going to end.

There is, however, one big difference between your freelance career and a mystery novel—*you're* the one who's in control of the final outcome, and not someone else. And in the long run, that's probably the greatest advantage to becoming a full-time freelance writer.

Index

(Italicized numerals indicate pages with illustrations.)

213